M000266462

Spectral Realms

No. 1 ‡ Summer 2014

Edited by S. T. Joshi

The spectral realms that thou canst see
With eyes veil'd from the world and me.

"To a Dreamer," *H. P. Lovecraft*

SPECTRAL REALMS is published twice a year by Hippocampus Press,
P.O. Box 641, New York, NY 10156 (www.hippocampuspress.com).
Copyright © 2014 by Hippocampus Press. All works are © 2014 by their
respective authors. The cover, *Death Reading from a Human Lectern,
Congregation in Background* by Eugenio Lucas (1817-1870) is courtesy of
The Pierpont Morgan Library, New York. I, 111c. Cover design by
Barbara Briggs Silbert. Hippocampus Press logo by Anastasia Damianakos.

ISBN 978-1-61498-095-7   ISSN 2333-4215

Contents

Classic Reprints

Reviews

Notes on Contributors 134

Editorial

THE LAST FEW DECADES have seen a remarkable efflorescence of weird poetry, to such a degree that we can authentically state that a renaissance of the genre is underway. In part this revival is a product of the upsurge of literate (i.e., non-commercial) weird fiction as cultivated by such writers as Caitlín R. Kiernan, Laird Barron, Jonathan Thomas, and many others (including the veteran Ramsey Campbell, who continues to produce outstanding work in his sixth decade of writing), but it also reflects the continuing influence of such leading weird poets of the past as Clark Ashton Smith, H. P. Lovecraft, Donald Wandrei, and George Sterling, all of whose work has appeared in new editions in recent years. That the best of this new weird verse continues to work in formal metres and rhyme-schemes is a testament to the power and effectiveness of traditional verse forms after a century or more of free-verse experimentation.

The new poets who have emerged in recent years—Ann K. Schwader, Wade German, Leigh Blackmore, K. A. Opperman—join such veterans as Bruce Boston, W. H. Pugmire, and Richard L. Tierney in contributing vital original work to this issue, and we hope their contributions will continue to appear in future issues. Boston, Marge Simon, and others have ventured into the hybrid form of the prose-poem, a genre I hope to cultivate in this journal. Writers ranging from Charles Baudelaire to Lord Dunsany to (perhaps the best of them all) Clark Ashton Smith have displayed the richness, complexity, and ethereal beauty that this genre is capable of embodying; and in an era when the undue austerity of the Hemingway school is at last giving way to a greater awareness of the purely sensual aspects of prose, it would seem that the revival of the prose-poem would be a natural concomitant to the revival of weird verse in general.

The contributors in this first issue, hailing from the United States, Canada, the United Kingdom, Denmark, Australia, and elsewhere, are indicative of the worldwide nature of the weird poetry renaissance. While the work we publish in this journal will necessarily have to be restricted to Anglophone contributions, we hope that future issues might include translated items from poets past and present.

Because so much weird poetry written today consciously draws upon models from decades or centuries ago, I have felt it a central purpose of this journal to reprint rare but distinctive specimens of poets, known and unknown, from the past. The Internet has made this material available as never before; but it still requires knowledge and diligence to seek out the best such examples. I would welcome suggestions as to what works from our collective literary heritage should be presented for the delectation of this journal's readership.

The resurrection of classic poems from prior ages is just one component of the educational function this journal hopes to fulfil; another component is the inclusion of essays on weird poets or on topics related to the field and reviews of contemporary work, whether it be volumes of poetry, anthologies, works of criticism and scholarship, or other volumes of ancillary interest. The criticism of weird poetry needs to proceed hand in hand with the generation of weird poetry itself, and we have in our midst any number of able critics who can perform that role admirably.

Spectral Realms realizes that poetry in general, and weird poetry in particular, remains a cultivated taste; indeed, the extent to which the reading of poetry has largely dropped out of the cultural lives of even well-educated people is a catastrophe of incalculable proportions. Poetry is almost always the first and in many ways the most intense and powerful mode of expression that any society or culture develops, and its revitalisation in our age is a necessity of the first order. If this journal can make even a modest contribution toward that end, its mission will have been fulfilled.

—S. T. JOSHI

Poetry

Spectral Province

Wade German

The fog is like a prophet's shroud,
A mystic whiteness, which obscures
The features of the realm in cloud;
And in the city, nothing stirs;
Its utter stillness makes all seem
Embalmed in outer dark of dreams.

Vague shadows in the mist appear;
My query passes through the veil
To formless shapes that shuffle near;
They pass, they pass, so gaunt and pale,
As quiet as the dead are mute . . .
Deep silence reigns here, absolute.

The Laundrymen

Ann K. Schwader

They trundle through the gaslit London night
With overburdened carts whose banshee wheels
Cry havoc through the poorest districts. Flight
Is fruitless here, & even sleep to heal
Life's lighter wounds comes seldom. When it seals
Dim eyes forever, little can be done
By way of mourning. Better not to feel
Too much beyond hard currency from one
Who offers. Takes. The grim charade's begun
Once more, soiled linen bundled high to mask
Still-cooling meat from conscience. With the sun
So far from rising, better not to ask
Exactly *which* anatomist awaits . . .
Or why this silent minion salivates.

Seasonal Affective Disorder

Richard L. Tierney

Fall has succumbed to winter's icy reign.
The Yuletide fires have died upon the heights,
And carolers have ceased their "Silent Nights"
As deathly chills enfold the frozen plain.
Down from the north the boreal Vortex flows—
And now, at icy Ithaqua's commands,
A polar cold assaults the frost-gripped lands
With howling blasts of stinging wind-whipped snows.
The Frost Giants waken in their boreal waste
To smile with still more chill the southward lands.
About my heart I feel their freezing hands
Groping with icy fingers, and I taste
Within my throat the choking of all breath,
Darkness, depression, loss of hope—and death.

Nocturnal Poet

K. A. Opperman

Leave me alone. The visions I would glimpse
    All scatter at intrusion of late-calling souls—
Scatter into the shadows like the imps
    That watch this candle-flame with eyes like wicked coals.

Leave me in silence—say no other word.
    For hearken I to voices hid from normal ears—
Strange, subtle voices that few men have heard,
    That sigh in crimson drapes through which the full moon leers.

Hark midnight's chime—go—close my chamber door.
    For open lies a blank leaf in this crimson tome—
This tome wherein I now shall scribe the lore
    My daemon muse imparts beneath the night's black dome.

O daemon muse! what have you dreamed of nights
    When tapers falter in a ghost-awoken wind?
What succubi have bared their pale delights
    Unto your lusting gaze—tell me, how have you sinned?

What secrets have you wrested from the crypt—
    What wisdom have you pried from cold lips of the dead?
What purple poisons from gold goblets sipped—
    And whither, drunken with such draughts, durst you to tread?

What artful sorceresses have you sought
    In moonlit gardens where vampiric roses grow?
What necromancies at your robes have caught
    As you have traveled those dim ways that dreamers know?

Tell me of eldritch things, O daemon muse,
    My raven quill rests on this parchment patiently;
This haunted hour of dreams, do not refuse
    To me the strange, nocturnal visions destined me.

Old Graveyard in the Woods

Jonathan Thomas

There's a skull with wings, and an hourglass too,
And a cherub who sings that our days are few,
And to weeping willows cling lichens green and blue
In that old, old graveyard in the woods.

Down that road seldom taken, there's nobody around
Where once they had the makings of a flourishing town.
Now the aspens are quaking where the walls all tumbled down
Except around the graveyard in the woods.

And there's a little of that place in you, my friend,
Where what used to mean so much gets lost in the end,
And where once we were together, there's nobody allowed,
And nothing mortal stirring in there now.

No flowers ever grow inside those mossy walls,
Whatever seeds you sow come up crooked and small,
Maybe someone long ago laced the ground with salt,
In that godforsaken graveyard in the woods.

Beside the cemetery once a chapel stood
Where people came to marry or to pray that life be good,
And now they all lie buried deep within the woods,
In that old unhallowed graveyard in the woods.

Foolish men once came around in the dead of night,
Just to drink and carouse and do what harm they might,
But they heard some kind of sound, now they'll never be quite right,
Best avoid that old, old graveyard in the woods.

Carathis

Ashley Dioses

Her skin of burnished bronze, so silken to the touch;
Her hair of blackest midnight, wafting scents of such
Intoxicating aphrodisiacs; and her
Enticing eyes of hazel that made weak hearts stir,
Belonged to the dark Sorceress of high Samarah.
Fools only would court this dark queen whose mouth is marah.
Her heart was ice within a cage of blackened bone.
Carathis was her name, and she would rule alone.

Inside the high witch-tower of her dark delights,
She decked her walls with hanging bodies all alight.
Her floors were red, her followers were all deaf mutes,
And mummies who attended to her brews of newts.
Emitting fumes of mummies and the blazing flames
Frequently filled her working space as, without shame,
She practiced rituals, with offerings spread out.
Her tainted mind had found for certain, without doubt,
An entrance to the Palace of Subterranean Fire.
A place of treasures and rare knowledge to desire.

Such sacrifices of serpents and scorpions
Soon insufficient grew, and fresh new champions
Were needed to appease her gods of pain and death.
Servants, friends, children were the same, for every breath
Could easily be stilled, for passage down below.
Reciting savage incantations soon let go
Her earthly limits, and she entered down with bliss
Into the palace where, awaiting, was Eblis.

He greeted her as newly hired within his ranks,
And offered food and wine, which eagerly, she drank.
He gave free range of his grand palace, and she soon
Surveyed every dark corridor. How she did swoon
When finally she came upon her long sought prize:
The talismans of Soliman that held the skies
And conquered all beneath them! Quickly grabbing one,
Her heart burst into flames with a heat like the sun!
Explosive cachinnation pierced the many halls
As her shrill screams forever echoed in his walls.

Night Stalker

Michael Fantina

On nights when these long shadows simmer,
    These spirits rise up from this pool;
Orion's great star sets to glimmer,
    It is time for the werewolf and ghoul.
They stalk from each canyon and valley,
    To ply their nefarious ways.
Such evil they gather and tally
      And chant their strange lays.

It is night in this curséd September
    That I track through this fenland and moor,
Though I try I can never remember,
    For I'm charmed by a potent glamour.
These ghouls they avoid me and tremble,
    As I pass them they stutter and cry,
And the werewolves fall back and assemble,
      And give me "the eye."

And I walk through this long ruined village,
    Pass this well and a street that I know.
I have visions of plunder and pillage,
    In some bitter winter with snow.
I can never recall or remember
    Though I've prayed to that one mighty God,
What occurred in that ancient September.
      So onward I trod.

Ah, these elms how they reach in their swaying!
    Their limbs like the arms of a priest.
Are they kindly? And now are they praying,
    For me, an horrific lost beast?
I trudge on by the side of the river,
    And kneel in a small muddy brake,
As these ferns and these reeds seem to quiver,
      Life giving water I take.

Then it's on through these fells and this dead land,
    And off to the gray, haunted shore,
And I walk on the storm blasted headland,
    To hear the sea's hammering roar.
Ah, would that I'd sink in its heaving,
    To drown all my troubles, atone
For those numberless sins which I'm grieving.
      I'm so alone!

On nights when these long shadows simmer,
    These spirits rise up from this pool,
Orion's great star sets to glimmer.
    It is time for the werewolf and ghoul.
They stalk from each canyon and valley,
    To ply their nefarious ways.
Such evil they gather and tally,
      And chant their strange lays.

A Weird Tale

Charles Lovecraft

Wisely Schacabac said: "The underworld
Is not for eyes that see for if they saw
The monstrousness then they would see no more."
Against this hint the parchment I unfurled,
Depicting cuneiform strange fiends that whirled.
At which it shook, and made me want to pore
Over the script and find and *close* their door,
Forever seal it from what They had hurled.
Anon I made a trip across far lands,
Availed upon this loathsome shore now set
As if I could not do the less, and met
And found in tunnel entrance in the sands,
A dead man there, the eyes burned from his head,
And I recalled what gnarled Schacabac said.

The Star's Prisoner

D. L. Myers

Through ragged bars, the vile star sings
Its languid song of deathless spheres,
While sightlessly I stare,
A beast in chains upon a bed of stone.

In a dank cage, it leaves me cold
To bask in its infernal rays—
Forever to behold
The endless blackness of its darkling soul.

In ghoulish caverns of the night,
It soars above my helplessness
And cruelly drinks my life,
A sacrifice to all its brazen gods.

And how did I become its pawn,
The victim of its monstrous thirst?
I sought for deepest truth
And found instead the death that lies beneath.

Emeraldesse

Leigh Blackmore

As though from some gem-crusted world—
Far distant, circling dark-hued skies
Whose limits are by gods unfurled—
I see the walls that do arise
In Emeraldesse, fair citadel,
When it stood proud, before it fell.

Within the walls of Emeraldesse
The banners flutter in the breeze.
Its soldiers march; its priests confess
And sail on fate-predestined seas.
In Emeraldesse, fair citadel
There falls a note, there tolls a bell.

The heavy-throated bells peal slow,
Toll ever on in Emeraldesse
Its fairness flown, its faery glow
Half-vanished now beneath the stress
Of warring kingdoms that do press
Upon the bounds of Emeraldesse.

Red flaring sunsets round the walls
And towers so proud; with such largesse
Endow the endless darkling halls;
So princes live in Emeraldesse.
But ruined now, its antique charms—
For you have fled my clasping arms.

In Emeraldesse you seek to find
Sweet life without me, but I know
That which you seek will only bind—
Your mind's dark seeds begins to grow.
And ghastly shapes around you press;
Your life will end—in Emeraldesse.

Black Wings

Ian Futter

At night, behind my dreams
I would hear them;
flapping.
Whacking their way
through blackness,
purposeless,
but deathless in desire.
Spiralling upward,
searching for surface suns.

At night, behind my eyes,
I would feel them;
clumsy and soulless,
wasted.
Frailty whirling
In arcs of desolation.

At night, behind gargantuan
Black wings, I rested,
coldly:
A shrouded anathema,
silently waiting
to smother the dawn.

Fortune Teller

Carole Abourjeili

Amidst the shadow of death she appeared
Her deadly eyes quivered with fear
She sat beside her self-divine
She chanted hymns I wished not to hear
My soul trembled in disguise
She sought my youth
She sought my demise
She sought my youth to grace her face
She held me prisoner in her foul embrace
She laid the "kiss-of-death" upon my skin
I beheld my birth,
My life,
My sins
My spirit lost in her words divine
My sinful sorrows did me entwine
I cried a thousand sinful tear
My heart bellowed in eternal fear
With her fragrant breath I sensed my death
She led me to my eternal slumber
She hymned
She hymned
She chanted my soul into her world
Amid the storm
One with the wind

The Stomach Only Tries

Marge Simon

HE IS DREAMING . . .

A beautiful woman stands at a window overlooking the ocean. She wears a gossamer fabric that ripples along her contours like ascending smoke. She is eating a peach.

"Once I was young like you, Robert." She takes a bite of the peach. "My body got the best of me. My loss. You can't fill the empty spirit with food, Robert. The stomach only tries."

Her skin is flawless. Her golden curls are swept off her neck in a pearly net.

"You're very quiet, Robert. Why?"

His eyes follow the tip of her tongue as she licks the fruit.

Three times she asks her question. Three times he can't answer. She finishes the peach, flings the pit at him. Disappears.

He is dreaming . . .

He is standing before a rolling mansion. A beautiful woman in a red cape much darker than her hair walks toward him. She is telling him something he can't understand. She motions him to come through the courtyard gates.

The woman seems happy to see him. She wants him to play with her pets. One is gray and one white. They are Great Danes, but he has never seen one before. He thinks they are ponies. They are too small to ride, so he runs around the yard with them. When he is tired, the gray one comes up to lick his hand. He tries to feed it some grass, but it runs off.

She brings him tea and sugared apricots. They make a picnic by an indigo stream. She says it is immortal, this stream. He doesn't know what to say. He smiles, touches her hand. It is a soft hand, but strong. Her nails are immaculate. He likes this. He likes to look at her.

"Once I was young like you, Robert." She takes an apricot, holds it between thumb and forefinger.

"Once before, my body got the best of me. My loss. You can't fill the empty spirit with food, Robert. The stomach only tries.

"You're very quiet, Robert. Why?"

He watches her tongue flick juice from the fruit.

Three times she asks her question. Three times he can't answer her. She finishes the apricot, flings the pit at him. Disappears.

He is dreaming . . .

He is running through a forest. Sunlight flickers in and out of the dense foliage as he runs. A clearing forms ahead. As he draws closer, he sees a beautiful woman bathing in a pond. There is an aura over this pond, the air is alive with pebbled light.

The woman nods his way and rises from the water smiling. "At last you've found me," she says. "I've been waiting so very long." Before he can speak, she is in his arms. Her hair smells like golden apples.

"Once I was young like you, Robert." It is a whisper. She plucks an apple from the air, nestles it under her chin. "Once before, my body got the best of me—"

Her lips tease the apple. Her teeth are so white, so sharp.

"You're very quiet, Robert. Why?"

He watches her teeth dig into the apple. He tells himself this is a wondrous thing, this woman, this apple.

Three times she asks the question. Three times he cannot answer.

She frowns. "I'm sad for you, Robert." She opens her mouth. It is a very large mouth that becomes wider as he stares.

In this forest, he could see no horizon until now. It is lined with razor teeth. In his nostrils, the smell of decaying fruit.

"Once again, my body gets the best of me, Robert . . ."

Audience at Sunset

David Barker and W. H. Pugmire

Exiting the onyx temple
I encounter the High Priest,
His face half-sheathed in yellow silk,
Two comely companions attending.

Slender of limb in satin raiment,
They might be slave girls
Or exotic dancers
Who move their limbs in dying sunlight.

The women bend to funeral pyre,
Where flames are fueled by bones
Of innocents;
And with this sacrificial flame
They ignite their scented cigarettes.

One acolyte suggests that wine
Is holy nectar, the blood of gods—
And then she laughs as if in jest,
And dances in the wine she spills.

Secluded in the amber palace
his aged consort is protected
from secret dreams and harsh realities
by the cooing of doves
carried on an evening wind.

The drunken girls come and go.
They could be whores or beggars.
They sidle up to him silently
and he extinguishes their cigarettes
with serpent tongue.
Staring long into the sunset,
he is deciding if he'll enter
the Room of Colored Glass
this final time;
the price one pays for beauty
is always terrible.

The silken yellow mask
cloaks half his face; I
cannot see his eyes.

One hour more of crimson radiance
before night brings strange music
to the distant hills.

As Told to My Infant Grandchildren

Phillip A. Ellis

My father's father lay within the stifled
and incense fuming room. His breath was fading
so slowly but perceptibly. He counted
the ticking of the death-watch beetle, timing
its marks against the silence with his counting.

His pocket watch was held against the darkness,
as though it's time that keeps away the silence,
and only it was stopping him from dying
with grim tenacity. He never ventured
a spoken word, but counted, always trembling.

The moment that he died, the ticking ended.
We paid the penny for the boatman, ferried
the body on the bed into the evening,
and buried both. The watch was also buried;
it held his soul, so intimate its usage.

That winter, while the storms were wild and tameless,
my father's father came again, as spirit
forever nameless, tried to enter, take us,
and leave us crying as a soul that's orphaned
within the winds beneath the eaves of houses.

The Hidden God

Adam Bolivar

Josiah Drake, the craven son,
    The son of Jackson Drake,
Was cast adrift and tempest-tost;
    All hope did he forsake.

Josiah Drake was kept afloat
    Upon a cedar ark.
Within the ark a treasure lay,
    An emerald in the dark.

At last, half-dead, Drake washed ashore
    Where dwelt the Hidden God.
A sapphire isle, a gloomy place,
    It was the Land of Nod.

Josiah Drake sat on the sand,
    And gazed across the deep.
His brother's death a noble stand,
    And yet it made him weep.

His skin was burnt, his coat in rags,
    And lost his book and sword.
He fell asleep there on the sand,
    And to the House was lured.

Ajar the door into the House,
    He found inside quite small.
And in the House, cat toyed with mouse
    Inside the bedroom wall.

A Herald woke Drake in the night;
    His horse was black as sin.
Josiah thought of taking flight,
    A race he could not win.

The Herald bore a coat of arms,
    Emblazed a yellow sign.
And from his hip he drew a flask,
    Engraved that cruel design.

The Herald dropped the flask athwart
    The toe of Drake's worn boot.
And asked him if he served the Court,
    A question that was moot.

Josiah could not answer him.
    "Well, from the flask do drink,"
The Herald said to Drake.
    "Then tell me what you think."

The Herald's horse then bore him off,
    And with Drake left the flask.
This hidden drink that he must quaff,
    What was it might he ask.

He pressed the flask to thirsty lips,
    Inside was nectar brown;
And turning bottom's end to up,
    He poured the nectar down.

He nodding dreamt a theatre stage
    Of dancing bones on strings.
The threads were spun in twists of fate
    That spiders know what brings.

One puppet's dance did catch his eye,
    The winged cloaked shape of Death,
Who tightly held a flask in hand
    To catch a man's last breath.

Josiah woke to breaking dawn,
    A spectre now the play.
His hurt was gone; his skin was wan;
    He shrunk now from the day.

The Land of Nod is stark terrain,
    Where winds forever mourn.
The endless rain pours down in vain
    Upon a land forlorn.

The son of Drake kept to the path
    That spiralled up the mount.
A garden met him at its end,
    And empty was the fount.

Atop the gate there perched an owl,
    Whose feathers all were black,
Upon his face a fearsome scowl,
    His claws bared to attack.

The Herald rode up on his horse,
    And stood beside the gate
To usher Drake, and what is worse,
    To seal Josiah's fate.

The trees were bare, no flowers grew,
    No honey in the comb.
The sky was black where once was blue,
    Aethereal the dome.

Within the yard a weeping girl,
   Stone-frozen there for years:
And at her feet there lay a flask;
   The flask was full of tears.

He took the flask in sympathy:
   To sleep his only goal.
He drank it dry to ease the pain,
   And so he lost his soul.

To nodding eyes the roses bloomed,
   Their petals starkest white.
Beneath an opalescent moon,
   Josiah spent the night.

He dreamt about the hidden House,
   Whose Mistress's name was Grey.
She had him to her room for tea
   So like an ass he'd bray.

The dawn came up; no rooster crowed;
   The mist clung to the moat.
Across the moat a ferry rowed,
   The Oarsman like a goat.

The Oarsman then held out his hand:
    "What have you for my fee?"
And hoisting up his worthy pole:
    "That Emerald would suit me."

The Herald blocked the ferryman,
    And paid him with a groat.
"Our guest pays court to Mistress Grey;
    Now row us in your boat."

Into the gate, his honour foiled,
    Drake saw no other choice.
Around his throat a serpent coiled,
    Until he lost his voice.

He shed his rags and donned a coat,
    A coat of pitchest black.
A silver sword went in his sheath;
    Drake joined the court, alack!

The Queen was grim, her name was Grey,
    A needle in her hand.
She woke by night and slept by day,
    A-counting grains of sand.

The needle pricked Drake's starving vein,
    And drew a drop of blood.
The price was such a tiny pain
    For such a blissful flood.

In dreams the modest House appeared
    A castle bleak and tall.
Shipwrecked upon the Land of Nod,
    Drake sheltered in its wall.

The nectar flowed in streams of gold;
    He craved it like a bee.
It numbed his soul against the cold;
    He loved it as did she.

One day he would climb up the stair
    To meet the Hidden God.
It chilled the spine and prickled skin
    To see the King of Nod.

Upon an oaken throne in chains,
    He found his forebear Jack:
"By turning wheel and grinding stone,
    I bid thee welcome back."

He bent his knee to Hidden God,
    And mourned the fate of Drakes.
A wolf-wind howled through barren Nod,
    A dreary sound it makes.

Josiah took his place at tea,
    The Queen sat by his side.
They pricked their veins each one of three,
    A kindred kept inside.

The hearth ablaze with dreams of fire,
    They wished their cups with tea:
To each of them his heart's desire,
    Whatever it might be.

Up in his room the Hidden God
    Was kicking up a din.
He would not stop till all was Nod,
    And every man his kin.

"I am Yᵉ Olde, Yᵉ Shepherd Black,
    Now give me what is due.
Thy father paid and so did Jack
    And now Josiah, you."

The Emerald lay inside a box,
　　Held fast there with a spell.
There is a word that it unlocks;
　　To you the word I'll tell:

"Four feathers lost old Mother Goose;
　　One feather made a pen.
The pen with ink four letters wrote;
　　The word it spelled: AMEN."

And now the ark yawned open wide:
　　The Emerald he beheld.
Its beauty was beyond my pen
　　That in his hand he held.

Drake slowly crept up stair by stair;
　　Like needles on his skin,
The cold did bristle up his hair;
　　The walls were closing in.

Atop the stair an oaken door,
　　An acorn for a knob.
He turned the knob: it opened wide.
　　He heard a stifled sob.

He put a foot across the jamb,
    Wood creaking like a ship.
The Shepherd warned the bleating lamb,
    Lest on the blood he slip.

The attic room was cloaked in dark;
    A candle shed a light.
A jingling sound he then did hark:
    The Hidden God in sight.

Bound up in chains, in chains of lead,
    Hung from a hook, his cage.
While from his arm a river bled,
    The Hidden God did rage.

Upon his brow a golden crown,
    The Emerald it adorned.
The House began a-falling down;
    The brazen Herald horned.

A full moon hung, ballooned with blood;
    The mountain tumbled down.
Across the island washed a flood,
    And threatened him to drown.

Josiah Drake stood on the roof
    To beg the starry sky.
And in the midst of raging storm,
    A Raven heard his cry.

The Raven's claws clasped to his waist,
    And heavenward he flew.
Of angel's warmth he had a taste;
    The devil had his due.

The son came home, his father dead,
    A scapegoat to a god:
A golden crown around his head,
    He was the King of Nod.

Siren of the Dead

K. A. Opperman

Waiting beneath an ancient, rotted tree
Fixed with a cross which marks the boundary
    Of the Forest of the Dead,
Her icy eyes are phares which lure the flames
Of lonely travelers ruled by amorous aims,
    Who would share her filthy bed.

She gestures with a finger worm-like, gray,
That burrows though the hearts of those who stray
    Too near, forgetting their quests.
Her purple lips whisper sweet promises,
Expelling spiders with each word she says,
    Which crawl adown her breasts.

Like moths that dare the burning doom of fire,
Men prove amid her pale limbs dark desire,
    A soulless, pulseless love.
And when she parts her curtain of dark hair
To kiss her victims, a wisp of black air
    Breathes forth, of Slumber wove.

Her lovers numberless grow limp and pale,
Locked to a kiss that kills, till their hearts fail,
    Lifeless against her own.
Yet still they rise, puppets of a ghastly plague,
To wander dumbly through a woodland vague
    With fog, where Death holds throne.

Beneath black boughs that arabesque a sky
Of weary gray, they wander on for aye,
    Through drift of long dead years.
And nevermore will they know lust for her
Whose long dead limbs dark magick keeps astir,
    To tempt whoever nears.

Climate of Fear

Ann K. Schwader

There is a wind made terrible by time
That rages through the raw Antarctic wastes;
Its voice near human, hideous with rhyme,
Suggestive of a species Man replaced
Too early & too utterly to mark
Its myth as more than whispers from the dark.

The sea-ice of the shoreline knows its force,
Likewise the islands only seals frequent;
Yet certain seasons signify its course
Between those haunted peaks that represent
A barrier best left in mystery
By all who crave a longer history.

What waits beyond is ancient past our kind's
Brief reckoning. Cyclopean & vast,
Its labyrinthine form reflects no mind
Arisen from the apes who shaped our past:
A citadel, instead, for spawn of stars
Light-years & lightless dreams away from ours.

Down countless corridors worn slick as glass,
Each wall inscribed in sinister detail
Depicting times no nightmare could surpass—
Strange battles, dire defeats—the wind exhales
With temperatures far less of Earth than void,
Securing both destroyer & destroyed.

Thus it has been for aeons. Sleep is death
Enough, if cold enough, to hold such things;
Yet recently some ape-corrupted breath
Of warmth has twisted through this gale . . . & brings
Dread dreams of waking to abyssal pools
Where formless horror mocks at nature's rules.

Some blighted day, when more than dreams arise
Released by fatal change to claim our place;
What stratagem, what desperate surmise,
Can save us? Or must we become a race
Emblazoned with extinction's bleak device—
Not from the stars turned right, but from the ice?

The Meromylls of Lake Lurd

Donald R. Broyles

LAKE LURD SPARKLED in the cerulean light of day's end as the sun descended behind a bank of Sugar Maples. Flecks of dying light, looking like slivers of escaping moonlight, bounced upon the lake's surface and then spilled across a group of growing amaranths where butterflies rested, their iridescent wings opening and closing in the cooling autumn air.

A vagrant wind moved across the lake, gently rocking the giant water lilies and shaking awake the lithe creatures hidden inside the leaves and flowers. Disturbed squeaks filled the air as a group of miniature human forms dove into the water and disappeared. Laughter traveled on the wind, and the quaint couplings that followed caused a further rippling of water along Lake Lurd's banks, gentle at first but then with greater intensity.

The scent of evening grew stronger as a dying gust of wind blew across the lake, carrying with it a bounty of copper leaves that settled graciously on Lake Lurd's surface. Meromylls continued to dive out of the protective cup of water lilies, naked bodies like quick spikes of energy, the sound of their voices now a dying echo of the light's waning warmth. Leaves of gold and scarlet became beds of passion as the Meromylls continued with their play, while the butterflies hovered above them as guardians in the night.

The other living things in Lake Lurd fought with single-minded intensity, with fervor and abandon as they broke through the water's surface, the sounds of their anger and frustration a bellowing chorus of unctuous grunts that seemed to slither on the water's surface before sinking back into the vast depths below.

White Chapel

Kendall Evans

The Ripper worships
In the White Chapel
Drunk
With bloodwine's sacrament
Flesh stained red
By dismemberment

Annie Chapman's livid womb,
Mary Jane Kelly's wounded liver—

Surgical knives
Have severed forever
All Jack's desperate prayers
And theirs.

Horror

Ashley Dioses

In dark cathedrals and woodlands mist-laden,
A horror lurks in realms beyond, unseen.
Few fae are pretty and appear to maidens—
Most of their kind are cruel, and ugly green.

A door can lead to their true territory—
The Otherworld, to which anyone might stray.
It changes Paradise to Purgatory,
And all cold shadows pave, for you, the way.

Night Visit

Charles Lovecraft

Moon crescents in weird eyes reflecting far,
    Large things whole voids across that watch the lamps
    Of evening light and spangle all the camps'
Bright companies, or of a lonelier star.
There lift dimensions of exotica,
    Mirrored mirage of lynx-eyed orbs, soft stamps
    In wax of night, and radiant silver ramps
In gossamer lilts the hair of nebula.

Anon the spectral hemispheres parade
    The other galaxies so meant to last,
In headdress of an elemental jade
    And pitched in streams of convolutions vast,
In panting vistas that the worlds make fade,
    And crescent voids in lurid strangeness cast.

Fairy Song

Darrell Schweitzer

Out of the darkness and out of the night!
We're coming, we're coming!
Bearing stout cudgels and knives of sharp flint!
We're coming, we're coming!
To snatch gold and silver and leave behind dust!
We're coming, we're coming!
Steal babe from the cradle in exchange for our own!
We're coming, we're coming!
To cut out your heart and put in a stone!
We're coming, we're coming!
You won't even scream until we are gone!
We're coming, we're coming!
We'll hide in your grave, make toys of your bones!
We're coming, we're coming!
All holes in the earth we claim as our home!
We're coming, we're coming!

Miranda

Michael Fantina

I dreamt Miranda came to me once more
Below night skies, the stars' beguiling net.
She came to me across the parapet;
Her beauty magical and her allure
Spoke volumes for bewitching, smooth amour,
To fill me then, anew, with sore regret,
As once again the age-old trap she set,
As she had done on many nights before.

We walked in shadowed splendor there that eve
And whispered words of love I scarce recall.
I felt her breath, her tugging at my sleeve,
And yet between us is that massive wall
Upon some river's dreary, ancient marge,
That we may span, alone, on Charon's barge.

States

Ian Futter

I am an absence, fading,
a rip.
A weep with no tears.
Duller than a shadow,
with a shadow's grip.
A shade,
ephemeral.

I am a constant, cancelled,
fear filled.
A lamp with no light.
A present, stopped
and a future, killed.
An ache,
residual.

I am a belief, doubted.
A blight.
A joke with no laugh.
A butterfly, trapped
in a pupa, tight.
A scream,
perpetual.

I am a thought, rising.
A spark.
A hope with no cause,
sputtering and arcing
In my inner dark.
A star,
insuperable.

In Splendour All Arrayed

Leigh Blackmore

Through endless starry ages have I been
As one who, standing naked, unafraid,
With palms outstretched, in splendour all arrayed,
Beseeches all to see what he has seen.

On alien world and serried dying sun
I stride as one who claims his rightful place,
Deep breathing of fresh air, with rapturous face,
Partaking of all things that have been done.

On earth I lived, in times antique and rare
And died, and lived again beneath grey skies
And witnessed many things with aged eyes
That made me will, and know, and then to dare.

And in far realms unearthly have I trod
As though with psalms, petitions and with prayer
Some strange and unknown deity placed me there
And prayed to *me*, as like unto a god.

Ethereal and celestial visions throng
My fevered brain, the deathless ages pass.
I see so clearly through the sages' glass—
These cosmic realms, it seems, where I belong.

Dark Mirage

Fred Phillips

High in its gnarlèd branches whisper leaves
Of scenes long absent from the view of Man,
That none of latter days can scarce believe—
Forgotten tales before our world began.
From gulfs remoter than the furthest stars
In space unknown by any living thing
Some being wholly blasphemous unbars
The nightmares that insanity may bring.

And in their wake by monstrous pow'rs unknown
Seethe phantasms that Death itself evades
Like black seeds that Infinity has sown
The fabric of existence to degrade;
Thus long ensconced from common human sight
Reigns unperturbed by Man eternal night.

In Cavernous Depths Yawning

Randall D. Larson

In cavernous depths
Darkness breathes. A massive form.
I betray my fear.

But I move on still.
Compelled to discover, what?
The haunter of dreams?

Stench of death's decay
Salt of blood, ash of the flesh
Lingers heavy here.

A voiceless oath calls
Me, unable to resist.
Its will stirs me on.

Sweaty blackness now.
I enter a large chamber
Presence slumbers, stirs.

My heartbeat roused it.
Sloughing off slumber it roars.
Dark cavern alive.

Sightless orb entranced
I wither beneath its gaze
My soul is consumed.

And ancient power
Satiated with my being
Resumes its slumber.

Sea Princess

Claire Smith

To them she's a story laughed off in the taverns;
They've never seen or encountered her:
She's a tale, legend, and hearsay.
There's safety in ignorance when they're in port.

But at sea she's there waiting for them to leave their refuge
There with intoxicating scents, potions, and her invisibility.
It's too late when the fishermen smell the salt-sweet seaweed,
In the air, as they venture out to the ocean in their trawlers.

She's in a gown of lime-green peacock's tail, sewn together with twine,
Her ringlets are adorned with a pink coral tiara.
She's sat hidden on slime-covered rocks, with cockles, limpets, and mussels
Clamped fixed gripped to them; and concealed by the cliffs' edge.

There she waits, alert as an osprey, eyes pinned to the horizon.
She dives under the waves and uses her voice to drag
The enchanted boat close, closer, closer to the land.
She smiles when it hits the sharp crags; and cackles

As its hull rips; easy as tearing a paper napkin in half.
She dances to the music of the fishermen's cries—
Their chorus of fear and horror—as their boat
Disappears, lost beneath the white-froth waves.

She collects a number of dead bodies:
They're grey, damp, shrunken corpses.
Sometimes she takes a few sips of their bottled rum
And she blushes when it burns the back of her throat.

She scavenges these leftovers:
Clay pipes, woollen hats, and silver flasks.
These trophies she keeps safely locked in a trunk
Like a guiltless smuggler's hoard.

She bottles their souls when done with their bodies
All in rows of watery, green, glass jars.
They whisper their appeals: *Let us go, let us rest. Please.*
But she won't yield; they'll be her guests forever:

All are stored in a deserted cave far from any harbour . . .
She peers into her oyster-shell cauldron;
And stares hard into its murky, brown, depths
With her single, good, eye. It shows her the quarry.

She's there on the rocks with her shell-shaped invitations to dine:
A menu with aromas, tastes, textures to entice, tempt, please.
Her table is laid with its plates, soup bowls and dishes;
Solid silver knives and forks, next to them, ready for the feast;

She'll dine well on her guests.

Necromancy

Kyla Lee Ward

Did you think to escape me by this ploy?
To escape *me*? Did you think you could hide
so I would not in season find you out?
And dig yourself so deep into this grave
that I could not exhume you, should I choose?
I must call this a poor and common plot
for such as you, and an unworthy death.
I see it now, and scarce can bear the thought!
To break yourself upon the mundane wheel,
to suffocate so slowly, day by day
beneath the weight of earth, who gleamed so bright,
who saw so clear and far! And did you think
that as all darkened, so you would forget?
By subtle transfer, I too would forget?

A common grave, and yet it has some charm;
An avenue of solemn, shading trees,
now lit by lamps as darkness claims the sky.
Such quiet neighbours, such a spread of grass.
White roses at your head, brick at your feet.
But false the name engraved upon the post;
I know the truth, and now I see that here
you swelled, engendered small and squirming things;
To share your bed with such profligacy!
But yes, I understand your real intent,

to gain annihilation through decay.
But we were strong, my friend, who taught me love.
The magic that we wrought was stronger yet.
Those sigils in your skin protect you still:
your form is whole, your eyes, they are aware.

You knew full well that I would not forget.
Not in a thousand years; such is the price
of this my Art, the sweet, forbidden Art
that once we shared. I bring dreams into light,
distil desire. On summoned wings, I fly—
oh, how we flew! How sang, how wonderful
were you and I! And even in your sleep
that memory struck, and so your rising gas
became blue flame. And so it was that on
this late Midsummer's Eve, I found you out.
You stirred to feel my tread upon the grass.
Then heard my voice command your corpse to rise,
by your true name. Remembered then, too late,
the dead no longer have recourse to flight.

But now, my slave, you must recall my touch.
The coldness of your skin gives me no pause.
As my hands play your nerves awake, my breath
shall resurrect your lungs, my kiss your heart.

Of greater value than black pearls in wine,
this kiss, and of more potency. And now,
as muscles twitch and tongue begins to stir,
I conjure you to speak, and not to lie.
This sovereign Art interrogates the dead
and such you are: your choice was made long since.
You abdicated wand and word, and fled,
left me upon the crossroads, crimson-stained.
Did you think that would weaken me? Destroy
the tang of my sharp will? Not for one day.
Else you would not have taken such long steps.

I cherished deep those stains upon my hands,
inscribing sign and sigil in that ink.
So vast our sanctum seemed, but I kept faith.
Through cobwebbed noon and midnight's blackened vault,
the lonely hours saw me attend the flame.
I starved and stole; performed such sacrifice
as made the one you saw seem but a game.
And now you claim that was the way you died!
That mine own blade had entered in your heart.
Whatever you believe, the fear was all:
your fear of what I dared. Had I not laughed—
but how may I say now that you were wrong?
How may I swear that you alone were safe?

How may I even wish that you had stayed?
And there it is. The knowledge that I craved,
Not from your tongue at all, but from my own.

Left in the shell of our vast sanctum, there
I tended well the flame, annealed my will,
so grew in solitude, in power and time
to fill it. Now my name elicits awe.
My slightest work commands a fitting price.
I have attained all once we dreamed, and more;
such wisdom as could only come with time.
The truth that at the crossroads was unguessed.
And not one part of this may I regret.
Perhaps, if you had stayed, we would have done
the like, but not the same in part or whole.
So do I owe you thanks? Nor payment, no.
To leave was your own choice. This one is mine.

So on your brow I lay my final kiss,
complete the work that neither could alone.
Return you to your bed and at each step
let first the borrowed fire vacate your eyes—
Dark gods, your eyes! I'd keep them so for aye,
as mirror or preserved within a ring.
But I am done, so let them cloud once more,

and let your hair grow thin and grey, and fall,
your sinews slacken and your belly burst,
and even those ink vows beneath your skin
must drain away, must drain into the dark
where all things coalesce, save you and I.
Peace shall return to this sepulchral green.
And yet I think that you will not rest well.
The silence once resumed, will not rest well.
I think at each All Hallows, you will stir.

The Asteroid

Richard L. Tierney

My senses, thaumaturgically aware
Of menacing throbbings from the cosmic gloom,
Now vaguely glean a pulse of nearing doom—
A Thing at which astronomers now stare
In fear to see the end of Earth approaching,
Advancing from the blackness of the Void
Of cosmic space—a ponderous planetoid
Upon this planet's regions fast encroaching.

Forth from the black, foreboding gulfs of space
A large and ponderous menace now draws near,
Unseen—until, in sudden shock and fear,
Sky-watchers see the Thing's vast cratered face.
I laugh—and watch its doom-trajectory
Crash home to blast Earth cataclysmically!

The Thing on the Mountain

D. L. Myers

Across the leagues, it stares at me
With yellow-orange eyes of flame
That seek some unknown, ghastly place
Within the tattered thing I call a soul.

With fiendish mirth, it scries the doom
That glitters in my haunted eyes,
While panic twists my fevered mind
And wraps my form in searing iron chains.

My life is forfeit, ever lost
To glowing cauldrons blazing bright
Upon the mountain's blackened side,
Where lurks the lurid thing that claims my life.

Note of the Executioner

David Schembri

I break the slabs. Halving that oak,
   They fall—so splintered—at my feet.
   I fetch another: I'm not beat,
I wipe my sweat upon my cloak.

I bring fresh water to my stone,
   By day, by night, my axe is sharp.
   I rest my axe, I play my harp,
I train, I slumber on my own.

I walk to work on paths so long,
   To carry out my chopping task.
   The days I wear the plain black mask,
I hear their breaths—foreboding song.

Some cower, crying with repent!
   The others fight and curse the crown,
   Until their necks are fastened down.
My axe holds death—and they are sent.

I venture home holding my pay,
   My duty now until I'm old.
   My leather pouch holds shiny gold,
For lopping noggins every day.

Ex Nihilo

Daniel Kolbe Strange

A cavern of dark is expanded into a cavern of light
and the baby bawls in its new prison;
the mother is numbed by analgesics
and intoxicated by this happiness
brought about by the arriving thing.
The father is proud of his accomplishment,
ignoring the state of the world: the overcrowded
airports crammed with students who want to fly away;
towering offices packed with suicides;
libraries filled with stomping madmen;
and hospitals crowded with fathers like him
who ignored everything at the moment of love
—and as the man realizes this, his own father
materializes from up behind him,
touches his shoulder like Caesar and tells him:
"You have done your part"—then he dies
and the son is horrified; his father
had always seemed so healthy and well,
and the doctors are summoned from the child to the corpse
as the new father looks at the son to see
the face of himself, already an old man.

The Den

Chad Hensley

I wake in vast obsidian great caves,
Stalactites crying phosphorescent tears.
I hear the chitt'ring of tentacled slaves,
I know the young of Shub-Niggurath nears.

I walk with glowing gems that light the way,
I see winged eyes flutter with maligned limbs
And gibb'ring, fanged mouths crawling in dismay
As taloned claws pull skull-encrusted scrims.

A stagnant pool belches before my eyes;
A slithering, robed daemon does arise
From the pulsating gore with blighted cries,
Revealing my true name to my demise.

An arcane fear tears gashes up my spine;
With bated breath, I flee this profane shrine.

Awakening

Carole Abourjeili

Possession of the powerful mind where it all begins
The dark side of life holding life's ruthless sins
Resting in my heart
Settling in my dream
Crawling up my mind
Until I wake and scream
Controlling my emotions, digging in too deep
Dying, the instant I wake from my sleep
A ruler of my dreams
It becomes the knight
Awakened by darkness
Asleep by the light
Like the son of Satan possessing Christ's tomb
Exposing evil sufferings through Eve's holy womb
Evil is being born, more evil every year
Until we all become Satan's no mercy, no fear

The Witches' House

Margaret Curtis

About the open gateway and the door
A herbal tangle grows, both sweet and fell:
Rosemary for remembrance of the war,
Wild lavender and jasmine by the bell—
And lilies bloom, whose pollen held in store
Might send unwelcome visitors to hell.
To knock or ring: how many strikes in time?
No matter! This door opens with a rhyme.

You hear a thud, perhaps a soft footfall,
But no one comes to greet you as you pause.
Instead, a faint call echoes down the hall,
A whiff of fluff, the scratch of sharpened claws
Convinces you a cat has climbed a wall,
Escaping hunting hounds with snapping jaws.
Whose fate hangs in the balance: theirs or yours?
Who dares invite you in? And for what cause?

A plume of incense drives your cares away,
Scent of an Eastern mystic lingers here,
'Mid dusty shelves of books that line the way,
Containing answers to both hope and fear.
Beyond these toppling towers shines the day,
A promise of Pan's garden at the rear;
And in between two bookends of bright light:
Dim passages and realms of restless night.

You strike a match and pray the wick will burn;
Swear oaths profane—and welcome candle flame.
You hold your ancient torch the more to learn
Of title, publisher, or author's name,
But none are in a tongue you can discern:
A thousand spells of fate—no one the same.
You might waste all your life here—die alone.
You glimpse yourself trapped here, a skeleton.

So through a battered door, your way to wend,
You feel the air suck in and heat turns chill.
The stair calls; you reluctantly descend;
A wavering flame reflects your weakening will.
You break resisting web, prepare to fend
Off bat or beast—no menu to fulfil.
Your eyes adjust and in this gathering gloom,
You wonder—is this dungeon or bedroom?

Your first impression is of comfort, rest,
With scattered cushions cast about the space.
Then turning sunwise—north, south, east, or west—
Altars surround you any way you face:
You do not dare to touch an object lest
You might disturb some ritual in place.
Dense frankincense and sage smoke fill the air;
You sense a presence though the stage is bare.

Then here rise visions, queer and "swift and sweet":*
The moon entrapped in crystal amethyst,
A cauldron full of apples, merry meet,
As shadows leap and merge in lover's tryst.
A chant sings through your blood arousing heat.
Magic enfolds you: you are fivefold kissed.
You dance as if possessed and yet you know
No demon dares to follow where *you* go!

A drop of blood is all of you they ask,
And all your lifelong toil will turn to ease.
You hesitate. It seems a simple task—
Doctors take more when testing for disease—
Yet you withhold, refuse to drop your mask.
There are no gods, or goddess, to appease.
You hear your name, a mirror traps your gaze.
Terror's blind rapture leaves you in a daze.

Moments pass. Vision clears. Shadows retreat.
An empty circle greets those that remain.
The drums are still and only your heart's beat
Completes this ritual. "We wax and wane.
You are our guest no more, so merry meet,
And merry part, and merry meet again!"
Two gleaming eyes of cat, or bat, or fey,
Propel you from this dark into the day.

*Percy Bysshe Shelley, "The Lovely Witch's Cave."

Museum Piece

Oliver Smith

A pale ghost in the land.
Alizarin poppies bruise her with pollen stains.
And fearing she will lose her moon-furred pelt
She runs home through summer fields.
Her spine ripples like the sea's white foam:
Under the corn, below green stems,
In paths stained with purple grains.
The star's eyes follow, bright sparks falling to the earth.
The blackening sky bleeds yellow flames, in multiplicity:

Like pomegranate seed amongst ergot stippled rye.
Promises are written in the dark spaces,
Concealed in the tump above Barrow Wake
She hides beneath the broken earth
And the moon casts shadows of black bracken fronds
Whispering with fractal tongues.
As ivy spreads fresh tendrils between the belemnites
preserved in the ancient sands.

She clutches her beaten bowl beneath the ground
Where bronze turns to verdigris dust.
Where strong green fingers push between the stones
And thin white fingers make their shadow signs
The transparent radiance of stars lost in time

Recorded in engraved labyrinths;
In the serpentine calligraphy of her mirror,
Reflecting there, from two thousand years away,
Her perfect face.

She cried a sea of tears yesterday
For hare's blood freckles on an English skin.
Now she smiles, having cast aside her pale fur;
Her human life and love.
Her fears at last are gone.
Painted on the hills
She left the echo of her witches' song
And resting beneath the museum glass,
She left . . .
Her perfect skull.

Kiss the Stars

Ashley Dioses

Liquid black darkness sears with icy flames.
In it I sink, forever falling, yet
Eternally suspended, all the same.
I am the light that guides, yet still I fret.

O loneliness forsake me, for the Sun
Does not adore me as the legends tell!
I am the Moon, She that most beings shun—
For gazes look upon me when in Hell.

Their hatred slowly brews as I show them
That night is everlasting, as is fear.
They cannot fathom that I am their gem;
The light in their deep darkness when I near.

Who lights the heart of me in my dark mess?
Who but the hot and burning stars, whose breath
Of languid warmth gives me the soft caress
Of a pure love that transcends even death!

Celestial lovers of the cold cosmos
Surround me and, though they are still so far,
Like lovely Venus or red Mars' Deimos,
I, in return, the Moon, shall kiss the stars.

Pursuit

Ian Futter

A spectre stalks and follows me,
in perfect pace.
With groans and gasps that hollow me,
It's hunger haunts and swallows me,
and shows no grace.

A nightmare grips and grabs at me,
from darkness, deep.
Suppression shakes and shudders me:
It clamps my eyes and covers me
in baleful sleep.

This vision courts and kisses me,
with basest breath;
seduces, slimes and slathers me.
With hauling claws it gathers me,
to looming death.

Afrasiab Down the Oxus

Charles Lovecraft

The streaming winds of awfulness groan loud
In this black hollow pit, and fill the dark.
They issue from some vent remote and stark
With crawling fear, a fiendish snarling crowd
Of travesties *below the ground,* a shroud
Cacophony to blither the mind's mark
And smother it with dread, like when a shark
Encircles a small rubber raft soon bowed.

By now the ghoulish night-winds have found throat
And surge up from the sub-terrain, and seem
To breed a life of shapes here out of dream
That one should not dare have, and like the boat
Afrasiab once traveled on and lost
His own sweet mind when the glass devils crossed.

Omens from Afar

Phillip A. Ellis

The smell of smoke had drifted, bringing haze
   over the ocean. Rearing up, the heads
of mermen read the sky; they sighed: for days
      the smell of burning eucalypts brought dread
      and omens of destruction. In the red
and sunset sky, the sun had set a globe
      of smoky flame, that burned an ember shed
with smoke, and smell, both seeming like a robe.

Their murmurs spoke of realms within the air,
      all fabulous in nature, myth, and kind,
in which they say the strangest beings dare
      to rear up realms of coral, that can blind
      when sunlight dazzles on it, and that find
a tool of heat that's quenched within the sea,
      that sends up smoke and smell, that chars what shined,
that shrivels flesh, and causes life to flee.

And so the mermen gathered, shaping thought
      upon the portents sensed within the west,
and on their meanings words were tangled, caught
      alike a fish within a net, their rest
      and leisure set aside the nonce, their best
and brightest thinkers puzzled, while the sky
      was filled with smoke and smell, like unto a test
from realms so strange they seem a bizarre lie.

Titan

Michael Fantina

I roamed a world where a titan hurled
    Stone idols from the lea.
And he stomped the sod where a wizard trod
    Who ruled this haunted sea.

And when he neared my heart was seared
    There by a pang of fear,
I dreamed once more of that distant shore
    Here in an ill-stared year.

And then a groan as if to atone
    For sins I could not guess.
Then he turned a girl as pale as pearl,
    In a long silken dress.

She called my name and a raging flame
    My heart seared like a knife,
And I asked most calm if she were the balm,
    To salve my awful strife.

She smiled and said that we'd never wed
    For she must play her part,
And further said that her heart was dead,
    For she owned a harlot's heart.

I roamed a world where a titan hurled
    Stone idols from the lea.
And he stomped the sod where a wizard trod
    Who ruled this haunted sea.

Lines on a Drawing by Hannes Bok

Leigh Blackmore

The waves wash out to sea with hiss and roar
Receding to horizon from the shore
Whereon the hunting figure, muscled hard,
Is striding proud, a seaweed-covered bard.

The barefoot maid he faces on the sand
Covers her breast and points her lightsome hand;
Her hair, aflame with moonlight, kissed with love,
Streams out, as does the light from stars above.

Does his grim visage portend some dark trial
Which he shall visit on her in a while?
Or is he in her thrall, her misty power
Dictating his dim fate in this late hour?

Beneath the Ferny Trees

David Schembri

My grandma, when a little girl,
    One gloomy storm cloud night,
Ran up the path around her house
    To see a dreadful sight;

Among the twisted ferny trees
    In shadows dense and black,
A gathering of terrors lurked
    Around a moving sack.

Foul lights lit out from their great eyes,
    A glowing, red and bright,
Brought forth the sack—released the prize,
    To slay with great delight.

"And I then saw the feasting beasts—
    The horror!" Grandma cried.
"So off I ran back to the house
    Beneath my bed to hide.

"My ears could hear the distant screams,
    And many tears were shed.
I cried in mourning for that soul,
    Devoured by the dead."

"The Hound"

W. H. Pugmire

I hear your ceaseless cry in tortured ear
As fate solidifies before my eye.
This Holland hill will be my moonlit bier
On which my mangled corpse will putrefy.
My breastbone is the bed of your icon,
Your amulet composed of antique jade;
That emblem formed in forgotten aeon,
That distant age of which you are one shade.
Ah, Sphinx of Hell, your grin is ever-wide,
It is the final doom I gaze upon.
No paltry god can stall my homicide,
No poetry from *Necronomicon.*
I take your savage kiss into my heart
As trenchant recompense for arcane art.

The Angels All
Are Corpses in the Sky

K. A. Opperman

The angels all are corpses in the sky,
    Interred within the wide, black tomb of Night;
And every white star is a cold, dead eye
    Set in a rotting face that has no sight.

With withered wings impressively outspread—
    Albeit in death-posture impotence—
The mummied angels loom as shapes of dread,
    With starry stares unblinking, cold, intense.

All human prayers drift past their heedless ears—
    Which could not hear even were they free of worms—
Each one a whisper that soon disappears
    In yawning chaos, tossed by stellar storms.

Their horrid faces haunt the starry Vault,
    Whenever I dare lift one fearful eye.
Sometimes immersed in desperate prayer, I halt—
    The angels all are corpses in the sky.

ᖬ Carcass, Waiting

Jason V Brock

Behind,
The past solemnly lies—
Dormant, quiet—
But with so much left unrelated;

Ahead,
The future desperately paces—
Implacable, rude—
With no expectations, and nothing yet to show;

Between,
The present tentatively cowers—
Unsure, confused—
All potential reconciliation steeped in silent doubt.

Above,
Everything abides—
Timeless, patient—
Distantly mocking any fears, yet without malice or hatred;

Beneath,
Nothing remains—
Staggeringly blank—
Providing no protestations, and with nowhere else to go;

Around,
Time and space collide—
Chaotic, emboldened—
As life at first wanes, then blooms, violently without.

When the frantic end rises,
And the beginning gently subsides,
Dim, cold reality breaks
As a new dawn is realized;
We are but a shadowed agent of tomorrow,
And the mournful sentinels of yesterday,
So while the moment erodes from remembrance,
We celebrate our decay.

Thus as season yields to season,
And ashes mill into dust,
We wile away each instant
With petty concerns, fears, and lusts;
Simpleminded and content,
We are oddly arrogant and proud—
Frequently lost and myopic,
Swathed in our insular mental shrouds.

We follow extinction's path,
Oblivious to our fate,
In a grim carnival of souls,
Joylessly parading;
At the lonesome, wretched last,
We comprehend, too late,
That each of us is nothing more
Than a sad carcass, waiting.

The Rim

Chad Hensley

Upon the ledge, below sepulcher plains,
White bones of every size fill chasms deep;
Great hulking saurians feast in bloody rains;
In the distance, larger leviathans creep.

An army of wingless gargoyles hold hooks,
Poke and prod the bulging beasts as they eat,
Led by helmed generals riding monstrous rooks,
The frenzy now a single, hellish fleet.

Amid the throng, a throne rises abrupt
Made from severed, decomposing man parts.
On the dais something beyond corrupt—
A thousand-eyed mass of pulsating hearts.

In abject horror, I avert in disgust
And then I see a shining tower trussed.

Classic Reprints

The Hidden Pool

George Sterling

Far in a wildwood dim and great and cool,
    I found a cavern old,
Where grew, above a pure, unfathomed pool,
    A flower of elfin gold.

There, though the night came lone of any lamp,
    Chill on the flower fell
A pallor faint, inimical and damp,
    A halo like in Hell.

Lambent it gleamed within the twilight calm,
    Long fugitive of day–
Malign, I thought, with alien dew and balm,
    A moon of baneful ray.

A breath of attar, fallen from the bloom,
    Made opiate the air,
Like wafture of an undulant perfume,
    Flown from enchanted hair.

A vampire bat, malignant, purple, cold,
    At midnight came to gleam
The honey that each petal would withhold
    From all but the unclean.

Goblin and witch, I dream, have mingled here
    The venom of their blood,
Nightly communing when that flower of fear
    Had broken not the bud.

But, lich or lemur, none remained to note
    The pollen falling chill,
A film on rock or pool, each yellow mote
    Pregnant with hate and ill.

None other bent to watch, within that crypt,
    The troubled water foam,
Nor knew, beyond, what violet ichor dripped
    From wall and hidden dome,

Nor why (though none came there to fail and drown)
    The troubled fountain boiled,
When touched in that dark clarity, deep down,
    A pallid hydra coiled.

What ghoul may come to pluck that flower of doom
    No witch hath rendered clear:
The warden of an unrevealing gloom,
    I watch and wait and fear.

It well may be a Form of death may own
    The twilight for a pall;
Till then I haunt the caverned air alone,
    With quiet under all.

[First published in Sterling's *Sails and Mirage and Other Poems* (San Francisco: A. M. Robertson, 1921); also in Sterling's *Complete Poetry*, ed. S. T. Joshi and David E. Schultz (New York: Hippocampus Press, 2013).]

Resurrection Night

Benjamin De Casseres

I slept, and out of their ancient tombs of tissue-plasm streamed a
shadowy host of Living Dead.
Gliding silently across the waxed and shining floor of my soul, they
breathed their breaths upon the emptied mirror of my mind:
And Terror and Guilt captained that crew.

The subtle fingers of the dawn brushed my brow and my soul flowed
back into the sluiceways of the old familiar world;
But long I laid in wonder staring at the wall, for in that night I had again
become the Things I was before my birth.
And Terror and Guilt were old shapes of me.

[From De Casseres's *The Shadow-Eater* (New York: Albert & Charles Boni,
1915), p. 21.]

The Angels

Théodore de Banville / Translated by Stuart Merrill

Greater and taller than our minds can figure them, through the immense ether where swarm the Infinites, and where the groups of worlds seem but specks of a vague dust, three silent Angels, intrusted with important messages, hasten their vertiginous flight. They are mounted on white horses of light, and clad in armor of scarlet diamond, to fight, if necessary, the monsters and hydras. They rush forward, causing the comets to flee, striking the frightened constellations, and, as they pass, brushing aside with their imperious fingers the manes of the suns. They are Malushiel of the fiery locks, who was the teacher of the prophet Elijah; Saramiel, the Shield of God; and Metator, the greatest of the Cherubim, he whose dazzling white beard floats to his knees; and in their midst rides the young Angel Uriel. While his horse is at full gallop the child Angel, clutching its mane and bending down, picks up on the road an insignificant little ball, and in sport is about to fling it, with his yet feeble hands, over millions of Infinites; but the wise Metator arrests his arm.

"Drop it," he says.

"Ah!" says Uriel, lifting his innocent eyes, which mirror the deep skies, "is it of any use, this little ball?"

"No," answers the Messenger, "it is not of much use, but drop it, nonetheless. It is the Earth!"

[From Merrill's *Pastels in Prose* (New York: Harper & Brothers, 1890), pp. 45-46.]

Three Prose Poems

Lord Dunsany

The Poet Speaks with Earth

Returning late one night from roaming amongst the stars I came on Mother Earth sitting all dark in Space, murmuring tales of her children.

"Dreams and battles," she said. "Dreams and battles." I heard her say nothing more.

I said to her: "O Mother, your sons have done marvellous things." I told her of all our machinery, politics, science; the famous inventions of Man.

Of all these things she had remembered nothing.

"But Steam!" I said. "And Electricity."

No, she remembered nothing, but muttered of poets and heroes. Not even mention of our Parliament moved her.

"Dreams and battles," she said. "Dreams and battles," and fell to muttering poems and crooning of ancient wars.

Mother, Mother, you shall remember us.

Rome

There is a road in Rome that runs through an ancient temple that once the gods had loved: it runs along the top of a great wall, and the floor of the temple lies far down beneath it, of marble, pink and white.

Upon the temple floor I counted hungry cats to the number of thirteen.

"Sometimes," they said among themselves, "it was the gods that lived here, sometimes it was men, and now it's cats. So let us enjoy the sun on the hot marble before another people comes."

For it was at that hour of a warm afternoon when my fancy is able to hear the silent voices.

And the fearful leanness of all those thirteen cats moved me to go into a neighbouring fish-shop and there to buy a quantity of fishes. Then I returned and threw them all over the railing at the top of the great wall, and they fell for thirty feet and hit the sacred marble with a smack.

Now in any other town but Rome, or in the minds of any other cats, the sight of fishes falling out of heaven had surely excited wonder. They rose slowly and all stretched themselves, then they came leisurely towards the fishes.

"It is only a miracle," they said.

A Walk in the Wastes of Time

I met a Spirit once in the wastes of time, as I wandered far from here, and knew him for one of the chiefs of the elder spirits of joy. And when I returned I went to his family, that dwelt in a land we know, and spoke to them of the spirit. And they spake ill of him.

I went then to the neighbourhood where he was wont to live, and there I spake of that elder spirit of joy: and they said little good of the spirit they knew.

Then I went to all the spirits of those that dwelt on Earth in his time; I found them where they were gathered in the fields whither spirits go, and to them I spoke of the meeting at night in the wastes of time. Some knew the spirit I met, some knew him not, and scarcely any cared. It was not them he had toiled for.

I left the fields in which those spirits were. I turned me round and travelled and came to Posterity. To them also I spake of my meeting in the lonely wastes of time. And lo, as I spake they all bowed to me. Lo, as I spake I saw them all kneeling before my feet, making me reverence because I had walked with that spirit.

["The Poet Speaks with Earth" was first published in Dunsany's *Fifty-one Tales* (London: Elkin Mathews, 1915 [not included in US editions]; "Rome" was first published in the *Lantern* (November 1916); "A Walk in the Wastes of Time" was first published in the *Smart Set* (October 1917).]

A Night with the Boys

Bruce Boston

IN THIS HALL OF EXPECTATION, polished wood reflects the light of panes both stained and leaded. The clock displays each second. By the bar a woman in a cloth hat sits with knees pressed together, face averted to one-quarter profile.

Richter came in.

We knew he was always good for an hour or two, so we called him over. Pass the time, we told him, tell us a story. At first the words had to be pulled from him like the last dabs of meat from a bone. So we ordered another round, another, until his words began to flow and fill the room.

He spoke of rushing rivers, diamond sutras, spinning tops with goat's eyes in their crowns . . . he told us of naiads and mermen, of forgotten cities of the ocean floor and how the hero Gilgamesh descended to the deeps, met the Submariner, slew an ancient monster of forty coils, and all this before Ali Baba could find the thieves . . . so we ordered another round and he told us of mountains, once living beasts when the land was molten, and how they settled to sleep and never woke, veins of ore now remnants of their massive bones . . . and he said that to this day each man has a mountain in his belly and a mountain top meadow in his chest, and all you have to do is turn the key on infinity, touch a lover's thigh, get a little drunk and wild flowers will blossom all through your cerebrum . . . and with another round it was the devouring womb and earthworms who build houses unsafe in any season . . . that's the way it rolls, he said, you come up in blood and you'll most likely go down in it too, what happens twixt the cord and the shovel is up to you . . . he laughed from the back of his throat . . . and he was losing it then . . . ranting on about shepherds and key chains and pencil lights . . . about '56 Plymouths and chainsaw licorice you could only buy in Idaho . . . until we had to douse him with "the mead" as he called it to get him to be silent . . . and before we knew it we were all dousing one another.

We sat in the silence, wet and dripping. The light fell through the leaded panes. The seconds fell. Above the calendar the woman in the cloth hat waited. Naked. Glossy and paper thin. Faceless as a pack of thieves.

[From Boston's *Short Circuits* (Ocean View, 1991).]

Reviews

To the Stars and Beyond

Donald Sidney-Fryer

GEORGE STERLING. *Complete Poetry.* Edited by S. T. Joshi and David
E. Schultz. Preface by Kevin Starr. New York: Hippocampus Press, 2013.
3 vols. $300.00 hc.

IN OPENING OUR ESSAY-REVIEW of George Sterling's complete collected
poems (including his poetic dramas), we can do no better than to quote
the first paragraph of the exceptional preface by the California
historiographer Kevin Starr.

> This three-volume edition of the collected poetry of George Sterling, at
> once scrupulous in its editing and sumptuous in its presentation, represents
> a long overdue publishing tribute to an American poet who has received,
> almost simultaneously, too much attention and too little. At the core of the
> Sterling oeuvre, as presented in this volume, are evident the triumphs and
> dangers of regional reputation as well as the near obliteration of the late
> Romantic poets of the fin-de-siecle by literary critics of the mid- to late
> twentieth century.

This addresses at once the peculiar problems associated with Sterling
and the California Romantics including Clark Ashton Smith, who seems
in his own case to have risen above them, especially the one of
"datedness," of appearing outmoded or old-fashioned. In his useful and
carefully calibrated book on Sterling brought out by Twayne in 1980,
Thomas Benediktsson also points out the problem of datedness in
Sterling's output.

> Clearly, Sterling did not understand the change in sensibility which
> generated Modernism; for better or for worse, he was of the *fin-de-siecle.* But
> in the 1920's [and also in the 1930s], fortunately for him, there were many
> poets and critics who shared his views. (131)

On the contrary, Sterling did indeed understand the Modernist change in sensibility; but neither he nor others with similar tastes much cared for it and its innovations, primarily on aesthetic grounds, never mind on intellectual ones. Fortunately for us, art and literature, unlike politics and religion, have infinite amplitude and variety. This explains the overall positive response to his last collections whether during his lifetime or posthumously.

As Clark Ashton Smith once expressed it, books are either well or poorly written: that is the bottom line, never mind the aesthetic or other theories behind art and literature supporting and informing them, even when their creators themselves do not always appear to be aware of them. Sterling's last collections include *Sails and Mirage* (1921), *Selected Poems* (1923), *Sonnets to Craig* (1928), *Poems to Vera* (1938), and *After Sunset* (1939). These books give strong emphasis to the fact that, after Sterling's death, his output did not vanish into the abyss of outer space.

Although Benediktsson's volume as a serious monograph remains almost unique in terms of critical attention focussed on Sterling—it came out in 1980, fifty-four years after his death and thirty-three years before the collected poems—Sterling's poetry, *mirabile dictu*, has continued to find publication and republication, even apart from the three magnificent volumes under consideration. As for the verdict of literary history in regard to the struggle (for supremacy?) between traditional and non-traditional poetry, the jury still is out, and probably always will be, whether during the years between Sterling's death and the present, or whether on into the future.

A word of caution: Starr and Benediktsson primarily discuss Sterling and his work in terms of American literature, sometimes also in terms of British and European (Continental) literature. The present reviewer will roam *ad libitum* across world literature (mostly European), from antiquity through the Middle Ages and the Renaissance on into the twenty-first century, and not just in English, American or British.

The set of the three volumes by Sterling follow in the wake of *The Complete Poetry and Translations* of Clark Ashton Smith (as also edited by

Joshi and Schultz in three superb volumes, Hippocampus Press, 2007–08) and *The Outer Gate: The Collected Poems of Nora May French* (edited by Donald Sidney-Fryer and Alan Gullette, same publisher, 2009), all similar in format and mode of presentation: hardcover (the French volume is a trade paperback), 6 inches by 9 by 1 or 1½ (spine), with no cover art like that for the Smith poetry. Whereas the total pagination for the Smith volumes runs around 1340, that for the Sterling runs over 1300 pages, thus remarkably close in terms of quantity.

Although French's poetry will endure at best, alas, as no more than a slender volume (due to her early death in late 1907), both Sterling and Smith lived reasonably long and fulfilled lives as literary creators, and both achieved quite a sizeable corpus of work, above all in poetry. Sterling died in his later fifties, Smith in his later sixties.

As usual (how fortunate that we can say that!) for Joshi and Schultz (and their many fine productions whether via Hippocampus or other publishers, whether anent editing or editorial matter), the three volumes by Sterling seem impeccable, very well researched, and beyond reproach; and they possess the full appanage of preface, introduction, and notes. Volumes 2 and 3 have the obligatory but always useful indices of titles and first lines, with divers appendices containing extra poems, selected appreciations, and a few surprises. Each volume has a different photo-portrait of Sterling, evidently taken toward the latter part of his life. The poet still appears noticeably handsome in all the photo-portraits.

A very nice touch: on the front cover of each volume appears the poet's signature stamped in gold, showing up against the dark blue of the cover's cloth, demonstrating again Sterling's lovely and regular penmanship. The reader would do well to read with extra care the excellent preface by Kevin Starr, who has long since revealed himself not only as an exceptional historian (whether general or specifically Californian), but also as a literary critic and historian of uncommon merit.

Volumes 1 and 2 more or less reproduce all Sterling's collections and poetic dramas. The latter became a special form of expression for Sterling. Some of the plays have made their debut on the stage, where they function surprisingly well, unlike poetic dramas by some of the Victorian poets, often marred by dramatic gaffes and other *bêtises*. Collecting the remainder of his poetry, volume 3 divides itself between "Dated Poems" and "Undated Poems"—and at almost 500 pages ranks as the largest volume, featuring a variety of poems in divers forms and styles. Sterling reveals here and there quite a nice sense of humor, sometimes overt, and at other times rather sly, although in general he maintains a serious attitude as creator toward his own profession as poet, even if he sometimes made light of it when discussing it with other people.

For the record we list the contents of the three volumes. Volume 1: *The Testimony of the Suns*, *The Triumph of Bohemia* (drama), *A Wine of Wizardry*, *The House of Orchids*, *Sonnets to Craig* (despite the name, a woman), *Poems to Vera*, *Beyond the Breakers*, *Yosemite: An Ode*, *The Caged Eagle*, *The Binding of the Beast* (some 60 poems inspired by World War I), and *Everyman* (drama).

Volume 2: *Lilith* (drama), *Rosamund* (drama), *Sails and Mirage* (this includes two of Sterling's best-known and best-loved poems, "To a Girl Dancing" and "The Cool, Grey City of Love"), *Truth* (drama), *Truth: A Grove Play* (a second version adapted to the summer performance of plays at the Bohemian Grove north of San Francisco and an extension of the Bohemian Club in the City), and *Strange Waters* (a pioneering but not uninteresting narrative about lesbianism).

For those interested in volume 3, please buy the volume, otherwise too copious and complicated for easy description. Although always competent and sometimes much more than that, in its traditional category, Sterling's poetry can still come up with the occasional surprise, humorous and otherwise.

As expected throughout this massive republication, pride of place goes to Sterling's often amazing sonnets. Little sequences of half a dozen poems or less clearly stand out, often augmented from one collection to another, sequences long since acknowledged and acclaimed: "Sonnets on Oblivion," "Sonnets on the Night Skies," "Sonnets on the Sea's Voice," "Sonnets by the Night Sea," "'Omnium Exeunt in Mysterium,'" and

"Ocean Sunsets." Overall, Sterling contributed to these sequences off and on from 1909 (*A Wine of Wizardry*) to 1921 (*Sails and Mirage*). Of course, the poet never contemplated publishing *Sonnets to Craig* and *Poems to Vera*, although they seem as competent and finished as any of the collections published in his lifetime.

Another point of comparison between Sterling and Smith: by our own rough count Sterling's total in these three volumes amounts to over 800 poems or separate items (including the poetic dramas or fragments of uncompleted ones), but his overall total probably amounted to more than 1000 pieces. Smith's total in his three volumes easily surpasses 1000 items. Sterling's poetic dramas (or fragments thereof) probably amount to 300 pages or more and bulk large in his overall output, occupying the same place (but not as large, obviously) as Ashton Smith's fiction does in his oeuvre.

We should preface our discussion of Sterling's life and works with a few remarks on the general state of poetry in the American part of the English-speaking world, if not indeed in other parts of the world, in other languages and literatures. Thanks first to the British Empire and now to the British Commonwealth, as well as to the prominence, if not the pre-eminence of the United States since World War II, English has willy-nilly become the universal tongue of our human-dominated planet, however unsuitable in a variety of aspects.

Spanish would easily make a better choice in terms of grammar, syntax, accentuation, spelling, etc., than English with its linguistic heritage divided primarily between Anglo-Saxon and Norman French, not to mention Greek, Latin, and the Latin-derived languages. As it is, Spanish must rank close after English in terms of people speaking it internationally. An enormous number of people speak the languages and dialects of Russia, China, and India. That is undeniable, but these language-users are mostly confined to the landmasses of those countries.

It follows then that, willy-nilly, many non-native English-speaking people have come to know and study in depth the historic panorama of English language and literature with all their bizarre and peculiar idiosyncrasies, from Old English, mediaeval, early modern, and modern, whether or not they deserve that prominence or pre-eminence. We speak here of things linguistical as they exist today, and not as they might have turned out otherwise, even if such speculation seems natural and often amusing.

When he died in his early seventies, Walt Whitman (1819–1892) must have taken some satisfaction in the fact that he had effected a wide-ranging and profound change, an innovation in one of the most significant arts, not only that of literature but more specifically that of poetry, generally more loved and esteemed outside the U.S. This innovation led to free verse and free form, a radical but useful extension of prosody from strictly metrical to a more flexible (non-metrical) approach.

This involved, of course, a novel and more "natural" approach to poetic rhythm, rather than that of fulfilling older metrical schemes, so that poetry could have a richer and more nuanced freedom of rhythm like that of prose. The term *vers libre* came into French in 1902, and then that of its English equivalent, *free verse,* into American and British English in 1908. As a medium, free verse remains close to the poem in prose, as first developed in France, and largely by Aloysius Bertrand, Baudelaire, and Rimbaud. Nonetheless, free verse and the prose-poem remain two distinct means of literary expression.

Let us discuss a little this new non-metrical approach, as evidenced in that revolutionary, echt-American volume *Leaves of Grass* (first published in 1855, and then appearing in its final edition in 1891–92). Incidentally, the shorter poems generally work better than the longer ones, especially the rhapsodical catalogues. The short opening poem "Out of the cradle endlessly rocking" remains an unusually distinctive piece. Each line is memorably varied and exceptionally incisive, especially for free verse, and here we come to the crux of the matter vis-à-vis traditional poetry.

The latter as its best really does make the metrical scheme emphasize the statement or subject matter, and in a way stronger than what free verse and/or free form usually achieve, by the nature of the words embedded in the metical scheme with or without rhyme. (Rhyme at best makes the incisiveness even more pronounced.) Because many poets at first perceived Walt Whitman's innovation as making the composition or creation of poetry too facile, they tended to disdain it as somehow illegitimate. But gradually, as more and more people used it, it gained acceptance and respect. However, the differences between traditional and non-traditional remain profound, if not divisive.

Opening up this new means of poetic realization represents a major step forward, whereby many people since the late nineteenth and early twentieth centuries have found a mode of poetic expression congenial to them. If at one time strict form and meter enabled people to discover the poetry that they were seeking out of themselves (say, from Chaucer and then Spenser as well as the other great poets in England and elsewhere in Europe), many people, chafing under the restrictions imposed by traditional form and meter, sought a poetic mode that gave them greater freedom to say what they wanted to say. They found this freedom in Whitman's remarkable innovation, and not just in English, but in many other languages.

Since his time, but more particularly since Eliot and Pound in the 1920s, more and more poets (more than a few ranking as great figures) have taken up and often excelled in this new mode or medium. For convenience we can use the terms traditional or non-traditional to designate poets and poetry all inclusively. The new, non-traditional poetry did not find at first a warm welcome, but gradually poets and critics accepted it, and it is now the reigning mode. However, following their own convictions, many poets have continued to write in traditional forms. Much of their best work often ranks in value next to the best work done by their predecessors. All good or great poetry demands considerable talent, practice, and labor. "Each verse means work, and none comes free," whatever the form or medium chosen. In a way free verse or free form is a misnomer.

Quite apart from the people who relished this new medium (that is, of non-traditional poetic expression), this innovation or revolution—more or less complete sometime between the 1920s and 1950s—left many traditional poets high and dry, stranded now somewhere between grudging acceptance and scorn or disdain for their apparent lack of novelty and enterprise. Some of these poets of an increasingly abandoned style of expression happen to rank as unequivocally great figures, even if not as well-known as their admirers would like. George Sterling and Ashton Smith at least in the U.S. (they do have their admirers abroad) remain prime examples of great poetic figures caught somewhere between two presumably contrary forces or conditions, the one traditional, the other non-traditional. Ashton Smith's popularity because of his prose fictions has forced attention back onto his poetry, and then that of his great mentor, as well as others of the California Romantics.

Thus, what might have become a greater general recognition for this group across the U.S. and even on into the then British Empire—Sterling already had achieved some of this, but not Ashton Smith as his protégé—became instead, to speak metaphorically, a fading or abandoned religion, with the former devotees flocking to the altars of these exciting new gods and their own particular cult, a cult that seemed to promise much more than what it would be able to deliver. Thus denied this greater fame and recognition, whether before or after Sterling's death in late 1926, Ashton Smith eventually turned to writing prose fantasies of extraordinary linguistic distinction for *Weird Tales*, *Wonder Stories*, and other pulp magazines of the 1920s and 1930s, whereas in the main the 1940s witnessed the extinction of such periodicals.

What then of George Sterling, his poetry and career? He had enjoyed that rare fortunate life that can happen on occasion. Born in 1869 in the former whaling port of Sag Harbor, Long Island, Sterling went west in 1890 and went to work as a clerk for his uncle Frank C. Havens, who had gone west earlier and had since become a real-estate magnate in Oakland. Sterling first lived with his relatives, but eventually moved to San Francisco, while continuing to work for his uncle, taking the ferry back and forth. He worked for him until 1905, when his aunt gave him his "freedom money" (so called), wherewith he moved from the

City and bought land in Carmel. There he proceeded to build one or more houses or cabins, and there he invited his fellow Bohemians in the City to come down and settle in that lovely region. It was he who made Carmel into an art colony.

Sterling had already met several well-known literary figures, Joaquin Miller, Ambrose Bierce, and Jack London, who became his close friends. Although he had already written some poetry in his youth and early adulthood, Sterling began writing poetry seriously around the mid-1890s, uniquely under the tutelage of Bierce. Dedicated to his poetic master, his first collection, *The Testimony of the Suns* appeared in 1903, and his last major one, *Selected Poems*, in 1923. Although strikingly different, Sterling as a great poet probably stands next to someone like Longfellow. To rank Sterling next to Longfellow represents not just a compliment but something approaching the truth. We do not intend in this account to follow Sterling's life and career in detail, but we must at least state that Sterling became known as the great poet that he remains (mass popularity need not apply here) but also as a Bohemian, man about town, musician, historian, critic, and columnist (for the *Overland Monthly*). Within its limits, Sterling's poetry is genuine and solid, as well as enlightening.

Compared to so much of the formless and often insipid poetry of today (too often trivially autobiographical), how refreshing Sterling's poetry appears in retrospect with its extraordinary tone and music, its élan and panache, its unfashionable poetic attitudinizing, its unfettered but stylistically apt vocabulary, its often unconventional subject matter and cosmic philosophy, even if rather unfriendly to the human species! Where does a reader or critic begin to do justice to such a lavish feast of imagery, sound, and sentiment? While continuing in the great Romantic tradition of Shelley, Keats, Coleridge, and Wordsworth, Sterling expands that inheritance, its depth and range, to include not just things immediately relevant to planet Earth and species *Homo sapiens*. That he like Ashton Smith often comes up with a negative assessment works to our advantage. Thanks to Sterling we become free of provincialism, cosmic or human; and the imagination like a jet airplane can take off toward unknown stars and shores. Such a poetic art and vision, like Smith's, are unique.

Let us quote some typical samples of Sterling's exceptional stanzas and lines. The problem here is that so much of it is highly quotable and impressive. We shall start at the beginning with his first collection (*The Testimony of the Suns*) and end with the last original one (*Sails and Mirage*).

From the title poem of *The Testimony of the Suns*, one may quote at random and come up with something well worth pondering:

> O armies of eternal night,
>> How flame your guidons on the dark!
>> Silent we turn from Time to hark
> What final Orders sway your might.
>
> What music from Capella runs?
>> How hold the Pleiades their bond?
>> How storms the hidden war beyond
> Orion's dreadful sword of suns?
>
> How haste the unresting feet of Change,
>> On life's stupendous orbit set!
>> She walks a way her blood hath wet,
> Yet thinks her path untrodden, strange.

From the title poem of *A Wine of Wizardry*, one may similarly quote at random and find such wonderful sententious lines:

> So Fancy's carvel seeks an isle afar,
> Led by the Scorpion's rubescent star,
> Until in templed zones she smiles to see
> Black incense glow, and scarlet-bellied snakes
> Sway to the tawny flutes of sorcery.
> There priestesses in purple robes hold each
> A sultry garnet to the sea-linkt sun,

Or, just before the colored morning shakes
A splendor on the ruby-sanded beach,
Cry unto Betelgeuse a mystic word.

From *The House of Orchids,* probably his single best collection before the *Selected Poems* of 1923, one may again quote at random, as exemplified in this piece, number II from "Sonnets on the Sea's Voice":

No cloud is on the horizon, and on the sea
    No sail: the immortal, solemn ocean lies
    Unbroken sapphire to the walling skies—
Immutable, supreme in majesty.
The billows, where the charging foam leaps free,
    Burden the winds with thunder. Soul, arise!
    For ghostly trumpet-blasts and battle-cries
Across the tumult wake the Past for thee.

They call me to a dim, disastrous land,
    Where fallen marbles tell of mighty years,
        Heroic architraves, but where the gust
Ripples forsaken waters. Lo! I stand
    With armies round about, and in mine ears
        The roar of harps reborn from legend's dust.

We pass by with little comment the *Sonnets to Craig* and the *Poems to Vera,* even if they have in abundance some excellent examples no less quotable. All the poems of both sequences well reward careful reading. From *Beyond the Breakers* we quote Sterling's literally ineffable sonnet in tribute to "The Muse of the Incommunicable":

An echo often have our singers caught,
    And they that bend above the saddened strings;
        One hue of all the hundred on her wings
Our painters render, and our men of thought

In realms mysterious her face have sought
      And glimpsed its marvel in elusive things.
      Her fragrance gathers and her shadow clings
To all the loveliness that man hath wrought.

The wind of lonely places is her wine.
      Still she eludes us, hidden, husht, and fleet;
            A star withdrawn, a music in the gloom.
Beauty and death her speechless lips assign,
      Where silence is, and where the surf-loud feet
            Of armies wander on the sands of doom.

From *The Caged Eagle* we cite an apt sample of Sterling mixing past
and present in a bit of praise "To the Mummy of the Lady Isis" (subtitled
IN THE BOHEMIAN CLUB, SAN FRANCISCO):

No bird shall tell thee of the season's flight:
      Sealed are thine ears that now no longer list.
      The little veins of temple and of wrist
Are food no more for sleepless love's delight,
And crumbling in the sessions of thy night,
      Pylon and sphinx shall be as fleeting mist.
      Bitter with natron are the lips that kissed,
And shorn of dreams the spirit and the sight.

Ah! dust misused! better to feed the flower,
Than grace the revels of an alien hour,
      When babe or lord wake never to caress
            The bosom where unerring Death hath struck
            And milkless breasts that gave the ages suck—
Stilled in the slumber that is nothingness.

While not generally well regarded, the poems in *The Binding of the
Beast* (mostly sonnets) are technically excellent, and not without a certain

bizarre (if unintended) humor given the subject matter. "The Crown Prince at Verdun" is a good example of Sterling's ready versatility:

By Mars his hilt! this is a royal sport,
    And fit amusement for a king-to-be!
    Surely the revels now permitted thee
Excel the poor diversions of a court!
Against the tireless thunder of the fort
    Thy ranks go forth as waves upon a sea—
    Puppets and pawns that move at thy decree.
A merry game, but mayst thou find it short!

Or is it as a painter that thy skill
    Favors the world?—daubing with red the snow,
As on the mighty canvas of a hill
    Thy cannon spread the pigments, till the whole
    Stands perfect, and applauding armies know
    The vision of the Hell that waits thy soul.

From *Sails and Mirage* we cite as our final sample another superb sonnet "The Wine of Illusion," once more dealing with misperception—or is it imagination?—without which our species could not function:

I saw One clad in opalescent grey;
    Who held a crystal cup within her hands
    In which a sun was deathless. Mighty wands
Shook as the spears of starlight in each ray,
And where they smote, the darkness was as day,
    And where they smote not, night was on the lands.
    Beneath her feet dead stars were strewn like sands,
And in her wings the constellations lay.

"Of this have all men drunken deep," she said.
    "Drink this or perish. There is naught beside.

This is the draught that fashions men from swine,
And though thy heart deny me in its pride,
Yet of my cup of dreams its blood is red
And thy lips red with my creative wine!"

Even if we do not quote anything from them, Sterling's poetic dramas are also full of endlessly quotable lines, whether in the dialogue or in the songs dispersed throughout them. We recommend that the reader explore them with care in order to discover the myriad beauties that constitute their essence.

In a very real and multifaceted sense we may doubt that Ashton Smith would have developed into the poet that he did become without Sterling and his pioneer cosmic poetry. Smith took what he got from Sterling, and adding to what inhered within himself (his own self-education in literature and poetry among much else), and from his local environment and cosmic ambiance, he developed it further, deepened and heightened it. As we have defined it elsewhere (the front flap of the dust jacket for Smith's own *Selected Poems*, 1971):

> Inspired by the example of his poetic mentor George Sterling and his two greatest poems *The Testimony of the Suns* (1903) and *A Wine of Wizardry* (1907),–long before the early science-fiction and fantasy magazines,–Clark Ashton Smith was creating an unique type of fantasy and science fiction in verse whose metaphysical and psychological depths have yet to be discovered, charted, and explored.

However, this definition applies just as well to Sterling's own poetry, although Sterling usually lacks Smith's cosmic ruthlessness or indifference. In his pursuit of what he regarded as the truth, Smith like Bierce takes no prisoners; that is, he does not compromise. Not that Sterling is a bleeding heart: far from it. Overtly his poetry here and there shows a more obvious humanity. Nonetheless, if his detailed and long-term encouragement of Ashton Smith (as revealed in the letters between them during 1911–1926) will always reflect great credit and honor on the elder poet, so shall his very own work, but even more, accomplish the same for Sterling as his own poet and person.

In a sense George Sterling, Ashton Smith, and Nora May French, along with others (we might include Bierce both as poet and Sterling's poetic mentor), represent California's "classical poets," more especially in their traditionalism, impeccable craftsmanship, and outward-reaching cosmicism, even if individually or collectively they still remain comparatively unknown to the mainstream (Californian or American) literary world. As Ashton Smith himself becomes better known, he will probably carry the California Romantics with him into the future, thus returning the debt back to Sterling and others.

How many poets have their complete collected poems published or, for that matter, republished, particularly when they thus remain relatively unknown to the literary and artistic mainstream of the latter twentieth and early twenty-first centuries? Unless very well known, such complete republication is rare, indeed. Without Derrick Hussey (as an enlightened publisher with a wide knowledge and appreciation of literature and poetry past and present), S. T. Joshi, and David E. Schultz, this collective republication of Sterling's entire poetic output (as extant in libraries) would probably never have happened.

As in the case of the complete collected poetry of Ashton Smith, the similar publication (in three large volumes) of Sterling's complete poetic oeuvre represents a staggering and long-term amount of sheer labor, whether involving original research (mostly in libraries public or university), conscientious copying, or textual comparison and preparation—even with computers, the Internet, and so forth. All honor to Messieurs Joshi and Schultz, not to mention the brave and enterprising publisher!

If Arkham House as a specialist publishing firm under August Derleth proved unique during the 1940s, 1950s, and 1960s, as well as up through 1971, because it published some highly imaginative poetry (usually fantastic and/or macabre), two anthologies, and volumes by Leah Bodine Drake, Donald Wandrei, Ashton Smith, and Donald

Sidney-Fryer (this last-named poet just made it under the wire before Derleth's death in mid-1971), then Hippocampus Press has far surpassed Arkham House itself in this one genre. May all possible kudos go the triumvirate of Hussey, Joshi, and Schultz!

Ligotti on Sterling

[We were gratified to receive the following discussion of George Sterling's *Complete Poetry* (Hippocampus Press, 2013) from Thomas Ligotti.]

THE SHORT-LIVED PHANTASM of Decadence and the perennial worlds of Romance have rarely been so proficiently and masterfully exemplified as in the life and works of George Sterling. Denied the Parisian milieu of Maurice Rollinat, who recited his macabre lyrics at the Chat Noir, or a fin-de-siècle London where an amber-tinted morbidity was too briefly purveyed in the Baudelairean verse of Theodore Wratislaw and John Gray, who glittered dimly among the more glaring stars of the era, Sterling created and presided over a poetic circle founded on pure imagination that required no peculiar time or place. While Sterling's epic masterpiece *A Wine of Wizardry* is known and widely praised among the cognoscenti of the fantastic and the weird, his catalogue extends more deeply and broadly in this domain and others, as Hippocampus Press has verified in its three-volume edition of Sterling's wealth of wonders he composed before his voluntary death by poisoning in the surroundings of the Bohemian Club. Along with his overconsumption of intoxicants and his influence on such eccentric successors as Clark Ashton Smith, Sterling seems excessively faultless as an accursed resident of environs both dauntingly grotesque and marvelously exquisite in form. As an alchemist of chimerical visions, Sterling is unsurpassed. For those who aspire to the extraordinary in their own writings or who find solace and delight in transcending this ragged landscape into which they have been roughly thrown, his work is essential.

Petrifying Poesy and Shivers in Verse

Alan Gullette

S. T. JOSHI and STEVEN J. MARICONDA, ed. *Dreams of Fear: Poetry of Terror and the Supernatural.* New York: Hippocampus Press, March 2013. 350 pp. $20.00 tpb.

WHILE THE HISTORY of supernatural poetry stretches back to the beginnings of literature itself, the list of poetry anthologies devoted to the supernatural is very short. Even more rare is a comprehensive historical survey ranging from earliest times to the present, and this welcome volume is arguably the most comprehensive—if not the first—published to date.

To arrive at this determination, it is necessary to compare *Dreams of Fear* with similar books in the field, with the distinction that "historical" covers several centuries and "contemporary" only one or so, while "comprehensive" implies coverage of most or all eras, as well as representative selection of the most significant poets and poems of each period. (This significance is here defined simply as the consensus of other editors under consideration.)

From S. T. Joshi we have seen steps preparatory to this collection in the form of his "Poetry" entry in *Supernatural Literature of the World* (2005) and his book of essays *Emperors of Dreams: Some Notes on Weird Poetry* (2008), whose preface announced work on a "comprehensive anthology" with Steven J. Mariconda. Better known for his language studies of the fiction of Lovecraft and others, Mariconda also provided a couple of translations for the book (Emile Verhaeren's "The Miller" and Georg Heym's "The Demons of the Cities"). The attractive cover design by Barbara Silbert features an effective watercolor by Charles Burchfield of spectral shapes surrounding a bare tree.

In this review, we will compare *Dreams of Fear* (hereafter, *Dreams*) to similar anthologies and relevant checklists, and weigh its achievement against its stated aim.

The Aim

The back cover blurb ensures us that "This volume will become the standard edition of weird poetry for decades to come." If this is taken to be part of its aim and not just hyperbole, then a further onus is placed on the editors to ensure that their selection is as comprehensive as possible.

Regarding purpose, the introduction tells us "if this volume has no other purpose, it is hoped that it displays the extent to which poets of the highest distinction [i.e., mainstream] have found in the supernatural a means to express moods, images, and conceptions that conventional mimetic realism cannot encompass." Accordingly, we will measure the inclusion of distinguished mainstream poets.

Defining the Genre

That our genre is *supernatural* is explicit in the subtitle "Poetry of Terror and the Supernatural"—with a double emphasis on *fear* and *terror*. The introduction states as a further criterion that the poem "actually depicts supernatural phenomenon"—the apperception of the apparition, so to speak, or broadly the encounter with an unknown that challenges our [science-informed] understanding of things—all of which is implicit in the term *supernatural*. This filters out poems that evoke fear of the natural, including death.

In addition, the claim is made that "To be a viable literary mode, the supernatural in literature must be segregated from religion and myth." I don't think I'm the only one who would debate this, and no real argument for its validity is given. As we will see, it applies unevenly to the selected material, not just in the earlier periods where the natural was not very scientifically defined. Perhaps the intent was to filter out whole bodies of Christian and other religious poems and hymns (including theosophical, transcendentalist, etc.), along with anything mythic or magical, Hermetic, or mystical. There is an inherent supernaturalism in all such poems; but even if they should produce a species of fear, they are preemptively banned (or deemed unviable) by this statement—perhaps due to the implied assurance of a benign divinity. Where this leaves modern mythopoesis—from William Blake to the spawn of Lovecraft—is problematic.

Put another way, the poet's response to the weird must be predominated by fear—not awe or wonder, which would admit fantasy and all sorts of other things. Of course, by analogy, some people like dark chocolate and some like milk chocolate, and again others opt for white chocolate, pursuant to their taste. Here we have a box of dark chocolate, take it or leave it! But implicit, I fear, is the doctrine that the only real chocolate is dark. This raises the danger of overspecialization through too-narrow definition of the genre—a special concern for an historical survey of this kind that purports to be comprehensive.

To be fair, the editors allow themselves an escape clause from their own criteria: "instances of non-supernatural terror have been generally *excluded*" (my emphasis).

The Scope

The volume is further limited to Western literature. If understandable, this is regrettable, since the need remains for a global survey. Epics from all cultures almost by definition include otherworldly (and frightening) encounters, including the Indian *Ramayana* and *Mahabharata*, to name only two. In the twenty-first century, with ever-increasing globalism and so much available in English translation, it behooves the editor to go beyond the traditional horizon of purely Western literature.

A Brief History of Genre Anthologies

In the introduction to his landmark *Dark of the Moon* (1947), August Derleth said he knew of no anthology in the field in the twentieth century other than Widdemer's 1920 collection of "spectral" poems (more below). Apart from fairy tales and children's books, weird poems had previously earned, at best, a small section of a general poetry anthology—e.g., Ralph Waldo Emerson's *Parnassus* (1880) contained "XI. Poetry of Terror," an idiosyncratic choice of only 12 poems by 6 poets from Shakespeare to Keats, among its 700 poems.

In 1919, Earle F. Walbridge lamented this lack and published a checklist (with first stanzas only) of 112 poems by 85 authors, *Poetry of the Supernatural* (New York Public Library, 1919), from the anonymous "Old Ballads" through "The Older Poets" to "The Younger Poets" of the early part of the century, including George Sterling's celebrated "A Wine of Wizardry." It is unlikely that Derleth knew of Walbridge's booklet, not that he would have mentioned it, but because the lists share only 11 poems and these happen to be frequently anthologized.

In 1920, Margaret Widdemer's *The Haunted Hour* (with 60 poems by 46 poets) was apparently the first all-weird poetry anthology of the century, but it was slighted by Derleth as "mainly spectral"—i.e., dealing with ghosts and haunting, therefore limited in theme—a disqualification that would make *Dark of the Moon* a clear first in the field. Besides being theme-based, Widdemer's book does not have very good historical coverage; and rather than being chronologically arranged, the poems are grouped into a dozen sections bearing such colorful titles as "The Nicht Atween the Sancts an' Souls," "Shadowy Heroes," and "Shapes of Doom." Nevertheless, Derleth reprinted a third of Widdemer's selection (20 poems) for *Dark*.

H. P. Lovecraft's "Supernatural Horror in Literature" (1927) listed only 21 poems by 14 authors—clearly of secondary interest to the fiction, but notable due to Lovecraft's authority in the field.

In 1947 came Derleth's *Dark of the Moon: Poems of Fantasy and the Macabre*, with 159 poems by 65 poets, an average of almost 3 poems per poet. Clark Ashton Smith and Robert E. Howard are given 12 poems each, followed (dubiously) by Derleth himself and Leah Bodine Drake (8 each), then Frank Belknap Long and Vincent Starrett (7 each). (Thus these 6 poets constitute a third of the book!) The most obvious and puzzling omission is George Sterling, and this was not rectified in Derleth's second volume, *Fire and Sleet and Candlelight: New Poems of the Macabre* (1961); its poems are mostly from the 1940–1960 period and thus it is not an historical collection, although it is valuable as a snapshot of its time.

It was not until 1978 that another significant (if small) anthology appeared, *Supernatural Poetry: A Selection, 16th Century to 20th Century*, edited by Michael Hayes (52 poems by 41 poets); and after another 27 years came *Poems Bewitched and Haunted* (2005), an attractive Everyman's Library pocket book edited by the late John Hollander (101 poems by 78 poets). Like Widdemer, Hollander groups the poems more or less thematically, in eight divisions such as "Ceremonials" and "Hags and Beauties." However, the introduction to *Dreams of Fear* dismisses both Hayes and Hollander on the grounds they "do not claim comprehensiveness." But upon examination, while Hayes is negligible, Hollander has the best coverage from the ancients up to the Gothics and Romantics (where he has equal coverage with *Dreams*); has moderate coverage in the later nineteenth century; and has the most even distribution across the eras—though he has only fair coverage of the twentieth century. Hollander's thematic grouping rather than chronological presentation may be a drawback to scholars, but is probably not one for readers, nor does it diminish the book's comprehensiveness.

Two other anthologies are worth mentioning only as good contemporary collections similar to Derleth's *Fire*, not as historical ones: *Omniumgathum* (1976), edited by Jonathan Bacon and Steve Travanovich (113 poems by 44 poets), which includes fantasy; and *Once upon a Midnight* (1995), edited by James Riley, Michael Langford, and Thomas Fuller (76 poems by 47 poets).

Dreams of Fear

Finally we come to the subject (or object) of our critique! With 143 poems by 97 poets, it is the largest collection of its kind in number of writers included, and though it has fewer poems than Derleth's *Dark of the Moon* (159), needless to say it covers sixty more years. The poems are organized into five historical periods, and we will review these separately.

For each poet a very brief biography and bibliography is given. These entries form a kind of mini-encyclopedia that will prove both interesting and valuable in pointing the reader to other works by each author, whether weird or otherwise. Among the various factoids, we are reminded that Keats and Schiller had consumption, while John Clare and William Collins spent time in an asylum—thus adding mental illness to tuberculosis (and poverty) as occupational hazards facing the poet! One wonders afresh what was in those 73 lost plays of Euripides, and one asks again what if Keats (who died at 25) and Shelley (died at 29) had lived as long as Goethe (died at 82) . . . Alas!

I. The Ancient World [i.e., Greek and Roman Classics]

The line has to be drawn somewhere, I suppose, and the editors have chosen to begin with Homer (c. 750 B.C.E.). While the introduction acknowledges the much older Epic of Gilgamesh (as old as 2150 B.C.E.)—whose curious fish-men and Enki's home beneath the sea foreshadow Lovecraft—no sample is given.

The four selections are mainly short excerpts from Homer, Euripides, Catullus, and Horace. Since classical mythology was part of their culture, they are all exceptions to the rule.

Hollander offers five selections from the Classics (Homer and Horace, plus Theocritus, Virgil and Ovid).

II. From the Middle Ages to the Eighteenth Century

Sadly, ballads by our old friend Anonymous are omitted—perhaps because no biographical details could be discovered. . . . The oral tradition proceeded the written, of course, and the impact of these old ballads on the Gothics is noted in the introduction, along with the suggestion that the ballad is "an ideal vehicle for the expression of supernatural terror." There are 18 anonymous ballads in our universe of poems, most frequent being "The Wife of Usher's Well," "Tam Lin (Tom Linn)," and "A Lyke-Wake Dirge." Walbridge lists 7; *Dark* and Widdemer each have 5.

Also omitted is the anonymous Gawain Poet or Pearl Poet who drew on Arthurian legend and stories from the Bible—sources that include supernatural elements. We might also expect to find something by Ben Jonson, Edmund Spenser, John Dryden, and Robert Herrick—more "poets of the highest distinction" who dabbled in supernatural subjects.

Among the 9 pieces in *Dreams*, we again have some major ones (Dante, Marlowe, and Milton) that are rooted in Christian belief.

The period is best covered by Hollander with 15 poems, ahead of *Dreams* (9) and Hayes(7).

III. The Gothics and Romantics

In this era, *Dreams* pulls even Hollander with 22 poems, ahead of Hayes (17) and *Dark* (16).

The most printed poem in our key anthologies for any period is "La Belle Dame sans Merci" by John Keats, and it is included as the poet's sole entry in *Dreams*. As for poets, Samuel Taylor Coleridge and Thomas Hood are the most selected, and both appear here. In fact, *The Rime of the Ancient Mariner* is the longest poem in the book; the introduction calls it "the greatest weird poem ever written," and elsewhere Joshi has termed it "a cosmic narrative of sin and redemption." It's difficult to see how sin and redemption can be understood outside of a moral or religious context (Coleridge considered himself Christian); thus the best poem in the genre bucks the book's stricture against scripture! Coleridge's other entry, the famous pipe dream "Kubla Khan," was regarded by Ambrose Bierce as "the most nearly perfect poem in English."

Sir Walter Scott's "William and Helen" (which translates Bürger's "Lenore") is mentioned by Lovecraft but may be the most overtly Christian poem admitted to the book, with its adjuration "O say thy pater noster child! / O turn to God and grace! / His will, that turn'd thy bliss to bale, / Can change thy bale to bliss." Needless to say, our sorrowful heroine eschews the advice—with ghastly consequences.

IV. The Later Nineteenth Century

In this era *Dreams* finally surpasses the others with 42 selections, ahead of Hollander (37) and *Dark* (36).

The most granted any poet is Poe (5), followed by the lesser-known Madison Cawein (4), who also appears in Widdemer and Hollander.

Dreams includes all but two of the 14 poets listed by Lovecraft, but offers alternative poems for eight of them. Left out (perhaps because it has also been ignored by other editors) is anything by "Ossian" (James Macpherson), whose "shadow-haunted landscapes" Lovecraft noted.

Among other notable omissions are the French poets (apart from Baudelaire), namely Arthur Rimbaud, Stéphane Mallarmé, Prosper Mérimée, and Théophile Gautier. Rimbaud's "Le Bateau Ivre" ("The Drunken Boat") has received high praise from the Neo-Elizabethan poet and scholar Donald Sidney-Fryer (who has one poem in *Dreams*), who compared it to both "Kubla Khan" and "A Wine of Wizardry."

Absent from the British Isles are Ernest Dowson, Arthur Symons, Dante Gabriel Rossetti, and sister Christina, Fitz-James O'Brien ("The Demon of the Gibbet" is one of 3 in *Dark*), Robert Louis Stevenson, and Sir Arthur Conan Doyle.

One of many mystical and theosophical poets barred for their faith is Fiona Macleod (William Sharp); Hayes includes two of his poems and Walbridge lists two others. Oddly present, by the same token, is "A Vision of Beauty" by Æ (George William Russell), which is arguably both mystical ("the veil was lifted") and Christian ("the Shepherd of the Ages").

The inclusion of Park Barnitz (2 poems) raises the issue of "bad poets" and an important question that faces the editor: how to balance quality with historical significance. The nihilist Barnitz is a famously bad poet, and it is only his extreme pessimism and misanthropy that won him a following. Ambrose Bierce (1 poem), though proficient, has been called "negligible" and even "trivial" as a poet by critics and considered himself *not* a poet, yet his historical importance as mentor to George Sterling and others cannot be ignored.

V. The Twentieth Century [and since]

In each of the previous eras, we may note that *Dreams* approximately doubled its selections (from 4 to 9 to 22 to 42), with a lesser increase in the final era, offering 66 poems by 40 poets. While this poem count is ahead of Widdemer (60 by 46 poets) and far ahead of Hollander (only 21 by 17 poets), it is also far behind *Dark* (102 by 32 poets) for this period—largely because Derleth provides more poems per author than the other volumes in general, averaging 3 per poet in this era. *Dreams* offers only 1.7 poems per poet in this era, evidently preferring to reserve space for more poets, honoring Smith with 5 (the maximum for any poet in the book, equaling Poe) and Lovecraft with 4 (equaling Cawein). Three poems appear by Ambrose Bierce's best-known disciple, George Sterling (reprinting at last the much-heralded "A Wine of Wizardry"), and three by his lesser-known disciple Herman Scheffauer. Walter de la Mare also has three, including the popular "The Listeners," which appears in four of the other five collections as well as on the Walbridge and Lovecraft checklists.

Some better-known names missing here include the Benéts (Laura, Stephen Vincent and William Rose).

Returning to "bad" poets . . . If not "bad" and certainly more lyrical than Bierce, Lord Dunsany (1 poem) was second-rate at best and is probably included only for sentimental reasons. Lovecraft, too, has been called "bad," which may be true of the vast bulk of his verse, though I think his best work excels and is well sampled here. Perhaps "honorary entries" could have been made for Arthur Machen, August Derleth (why not?!), Lin Carter, and L. Sprague de Camp—if only to recognize their significant extra-poetic contributions to imaginative literature.

Women Poets

A special note is needed on women authors. Women remain a small minority in the genre, but this can only be helped by including more women in a book such as this. *Dreams* has 93 men and only 4 women authors (Mary Robinson, Dora Sigerson Shorter, Katharine Tynan, Ann K. Schwader). It's a pity more were not selected.

Older names that come to mind are Ann Radcliffe, Christina Rossetti, Emily Dickinson, Elizabeth Barrett Browning, Nora May French (a Hippocampus Press poet), Jane Barlow, Amy Lowell, Edna St. Vincent Millay, and Theodosia Garrison. Insofar as several of these are also mainstream poets, there would be double reason to include them. Leah Bodine Drake's *A Hornbook for Witches* was published by Arkham House (1950; an audiobook was recorded by Vincent Price in 1976), and she was the most published woman poet in the classic *Weird Tales*, followed by Lilith Lorraine—both absent here.

More recent names include Ardath Mayhar, Charlee Jacob, Denise Dumars, Janet Fox, Janet Yolen, and Marge Simon, but my knowledge is admittedly limited.

Conclusion

To summarize our comparative study: while Hollander's 2005 book has better or equal coverage in the first three historical periods, *Dreams of Fear* has far superior coverage from the critical later nineteenth century to the present. Its chronological arrangement and notes on authors distinguish *Dreams* as a better tool for scholars and those who want to pursue authors they enjoy.

On the other hand, the aim to be comprehensive has required our editors to reach into the ancient and medieval worlds, where it is not possible to impose a too-limited definition of the supernatural genre based on what we may now think, in theory, it should be.

The inclusion of mainstream authors does lend credence to the genre, but more importantly it demonstrates the universality of the supernatural impulse. Other editors have also shown evidence of this, as mentioned. Notable poets "introduced" by *Dreams* include Catullus, Euripides, Marlowe, and Dante Alighieri; John Gay, William Collins, Mary Robinson, Schiller, Nathan Drake, John Clare, Æ, Oliver Wendell Holmes, Thomas

Bailey Aldrich, Conrad Aiken, and Robert W. Service. Among the "discoveries" are Emile Verhaeren, Christopher Brennan, Scheffauer, and Georg Heym. None of these authors appear in the other five anthologies.

I have quibbled over definitions, questioned criteria, pointed out transgressions and omissions, and warned at too narrow a conception of *supernatural*. (In self-review, I have also been good: I raised the banners of *l'égalité des sexes* and of *un monde*, but pocketed the more controversial red flag of *vers libre*–for another time . . .)

The fact remains that, when all is said and done, Joshi and Mariconda have done a really admirable job. They have exercised care and displayed both good taste and scholarship in providing an excellent sampling of the best poetry in the field, including authors that are best known within in the genre as well as mainstream authors who have merely dabbled in it. As a boon for their labors, we have a treasure beyond compare that will provide countless hours of entertaining reading and re-reading—and a guaranteed glimpse of the *outré*.

One could only ask for more! At only 0.7" thick, 350 pages, and 97 poets, it is *far* too thin a collection for so wide a range. The collegiate Norton's average of three poems per poet seems a good rule of thumb, and one might easily ask for 25–50 additional poets, just to be *more* comprehensive. In this age of print-on-demand there is reduced risk of producing a book of 400 or even 500 pages: *that* would truly have been a worthy standard "for decades to come."

Notes on Contributors

Carole Abourjeili started writing poetry in Arabic and French in Lebanon; then, a few years after migrating to Australia at age twelve, she began writing in English. Most of her poems deal with the supernatural and what lies beyond the known: "Each poem is a piece of my soul that I like to share with the world. For me, writing is a place where I find inner peace and connection with the Divine."

David Barker is a poet and short story writer who has written several novels but so far published only one: *Death at the Flea Circus* (Bottle of Smoke Press, 2011). Recently, he and W. H. Pugmire collaborated on a Lovecraftian novella, *The Revenant of Rebecca Pascal* (Dark Renaissance Books, 2014).

Leigh Blackmore was second president of the Australian Horror Writers Association. He has edited *Terror Australis: Best Australian Horror* (Coronet, 1993) and *Midnight Echo 5* (AHWA, 2011), and has written *Spores from Sharnoth & Other Madnesses* (P'rea Press, 3rd ed. 2013). Leigh is a nominee for the SFPA's Rhysling Award for Best Long Poem and a four-time nominee for Australia's Ditmar Award.

Adam Bolivar is a native of Boston. His weird fiction has appeared in *Nameless*, the Lovecraft eZine, the Freezine of Fantasy & Science Fiction, and in anthologies published by Chaosium and Eraserhead Press. Now residing in Portland, Oregon, Adam is the resident playwright for the CastIron Carousel Marionette Troupe.

Bruce Boston is the author of fifty books and chapbooks. His writing has received the Bram Stoker Award, a Pushcart Prize, the *Asimov's* Readers Award, the Gothic Readers Choice Award, the Balticon Poetry Award, and the Grandmaster Award of the Science Fiction Poetry Association.

Jason V Brock is an award-winning writer, editor, filmmaker, composer, and artist. He has been widely published online and in comic books, magazines, and anthologies such as *Butcher Knives & Body Counts, Fungi,*

Weird Fiction Review, Fangoria, and others. *Simulacrum and Other Possible Realities* (Hippocampus Press), his first story collection, appeared in 2013.

Daniel R. Broyles has always been an admirer of Clark Ashton Smith and Lord Dunsany. He began writing a series of prose poems, in the early 1980s, which were published in places such as *Nyctalops* and *Eldritch Tales.* He recently started writing again and is now working on a collection of prose poems and a novel.

Margaret Curtis (MCA) is a witch, writer, artist, healer and activist, living in Wollongong, New South Wales, Australia. Published in magazines and anthologies, in print and online, she is the author of four collections of poetry. Her poem "A Deathless Love" appeared in *Midnight Echo* No 5 (AHWA, 2011).

Ashley Dioses is a writer of dark fiction and poetry from Southern California. She is working on her first book of weird poetry. One of her poems will appear in *Weird Fiction Review* (2014), and two will appear in K. A. Opperman's *The Crimson Tome* (Hippocampus Press, 2015).

Phillip A. Ellis is an Australian poet, critic, and scholar. His work includes *The Flayed Man, Symptoms Positive and Negative, Arkham Monologues,* and *Four Ballads on the Crawling Chaos.* He edits *Melaleuca,* and he also studies community services.

Poems by **Kendall Evans** have appeared in *Weird Tales, Analog, Asimov's,* and other magazines. His stories have appeared in *Amazing, Weirdbook, Fantastic,* and elsewhere. His novel *The Rings of Ganymede,* a ring cycle in the tradition of Wagner's operas and Tolkien's *Lord of the Rings,* is now available (Alban Lake Books, 2014).

Michael Fantina has had numerous poems published in North America, the United Kingdom, and Australia. Three of his chapbooks are currently available from Rainfall Books in the UK: *Sirens and Silver, Flowers of Nithon* (25 Lovecraftian sonnets), and *This Haunted Sea.*

Ian Futter began writing stories and poems in his childhood, but it is only lately that he has started to share them. One of his poems will appear in Jason V Brock's anthology *The Darke Phantastique* (Cycatrix Press, 2014), and Ian will continue to produce dark fiction for admirers of the surreal.

Wade German's poems have appeared in numerous journals and anthologies, including *Dreams and Nightmares, Nameless, Phantom Drift, Space and Time, Weird Fiction Review, Avatars of Wizardry* (P'rea Press, 2012), and the forthcoming *A Darke Phantastique* (Cycatrix Press, 2014). His first poetry collection, *Dreams from a Dark Nebula*, is forthcoming from Hippocampus Press.

Alan Gullette is a poet and author whose work has appeared in three dozen amateur and small-press publications, including *Arkham Sampler, Crypt of Cthulhu, Cthulhu Codex, Etchings and Odysseys, Nyctalops*, and *Studies in Weird Fiction*. His omnibus *Intimations of Unreality* (Hippocampus Press, 2012) is in print.

Bram Stoker Award–nominated author **Chad Hensley** had his first book of poetry, *Embrace the Hideous Immaculate* (Raw Dog Screaming Press), published in May 2014. His poetry has received honorable mentions in *Year's Best Fantasy and Horror* as well as being nominated for the Science Fiction Poetry Association's Rhysling Award.

Randall D. Larson began writing weird fiction in the 1970s with stories, most with Lovecraftian angles, appearing in a number of small-press terror tale tomes. Recently, Larson has explored the format of haiku, corrupted into what he calls Cthaiku, in delineating the weird sense of horror in this poetic pattern.

Charles Lovecraft created P'rea Press (www.preapress.com) to publish weird, fantastic, and supernatural poetry and nonfiction. An admirer of formalist verse, he seeks to foster and keep alive that rich ongoing tradition. His work has appeared in *Nyctalops, Fantasy Tales*, and *Weird Fiction Review*, and a sonnet cycle is forthcoming in *Black Wings IV* (PS Publishing, 2015).

D. L. Myers's poetry has appeared in the *Absent Willow Review* and *Dark River Press*. His influences include Lovecraft, Smith, Howard, Sterling, Blackwood, and Machen. He dwells among the mist-shrouded hills and farms of the Skagit valley in the Pacific Northwest with his partner and four were-dachshunds.

K. A. Opperman is a writer of dark fiction and poetry from Southern California. His first book, *The Crimson Tome*, a collection of weird and horrific verse largely inspired by such luminaries as George Sterling, Clark Ashton Smith, H. P. Lovecraft, and David Park Barnitz, is forthcoming in 2015 from Hippocampus Press.

Fred Phillips's first collection of poetry, *From the Cauldron*, was published by Hippocampus Press in 2010; a second collection, *Winds from Sheol*, is underway. He has been published in the *Cimmerian, Studies in the Fantastic, Weird Fiction Review*, and elsewhere.

W. H. Pugmire likes to follow Poe's example and plant poetry into his weird fiction. His first sonnet sequence, "Songs of Sesqua Valley," appeared in *Sesqua Valley and Other Haunts* (Delirium Books, 2003). He is nigh working on "Sonnets of an Eldritch Bent."

David Schembri has been published in several print anthologies and magazines. His two poems, "The Lord and Reins Alone" and "The Torturers' Oath," will be appearing in a forthcoming anthology from Rainfall Books.

Ann K. Schwader's most recent collection is *Twisted in Dream* (Hippocampus Press, 2011). Her *Wild Hunt of the Stars* (Sam's Dot, 2010) was a Bram Stoker Award finalist. She is also a 2010 Rhysling Award winner. Ann lives and writes in Colorado.

Darrell Schweitzer is a short story writer and novelist, and former co-editor of *Weird Tales*. He has published much humorous Lovecraftian verse (*Non Compost Mentis* [Zadok Allen, 1993] et al.) and also has two serious poetry collections in print, *Groping Toward the Light* (Wildside Press, 2000) and *Ghosts of Past and Future* (Wildside Press, 2008).

Donald Sidney-Fryer is the author of *Songs and Sonnets Atlantean* (Arkham House, 1971), *Emperor of Dreams: A Clark Ashton Smith Bibliography* (Donald M. Grant, 1978), *The Atlantis Fragments* (Hippocampus Press, 2009), and many other volumes. He has edited Smith's *Poems in Prose* (Arkham House, 1965) and written many books and articles on California poets.

Marge Simon is a past president of the SFPA and editor of Star*Line. A former 1995 Best Long Poem Rhysling winner, she won the Bram Stoker Award for superior achievement in poetry (2008, 2012, 2014), the Strange Horizons Readers Award (2010), and the SFPA Dwarf Stars Award for short poetry (2012). Her flash fiction has appeared in *Daily Science Fiction, Vestal Review,* and elsewhere.

Claire Smith has two short stories published in anthologies, by Inkerman Press, "Cells" in *Loss* and "The Scenery" in *Cold Turkey* (both 2009). She worked as a research assistant at the University of Gloucestershire (2004-11) and has an M.A. in English from the Open University. She lives in Cheltenham, UK.

Oliver Smith's writing has appeared in anthologies published by the Inkerman Press, Ex Occidente Press, and Dark Hall Press.

Daniel Kolbe Strange is a freelance writer living in Denmark. He recently received his master's degree in English from Aarhus University, writing his thesis on the weird fiction of Edgar Allan Poe, H. P. Lovecraft, and Thomas Ligotti.

Verse by Providence native **Jonathan Thomas** has consisted mostly of lyrics for country singer Angel Dean, Manhattan bands Escape by Ostrich and Fish & Roses, Swedish quartet scumCrown, and his own Septimania. His prose collections include *Midnight Call* (2008), *Tempting Providence* (2010), and *Thirteen Conjurations* (2013; all from Hippocampus Press).

Richard L. Tierney's *Collected Poems* appeared from Arkham House in 1981. A later volume of poetry was published as *Savage Menace and Other Poems of Horror* (P'rea Press, 2010). Tierney is also the author of *The Winds of Zarr* (Silver Scarab Press, 1975), *The House of the Toad* (Fedogan & Bremer, 1993), and many other works of horror and fantasy fiction.

Kyla Lee Ward's latest release is *The Land of Bad Dreams* (P'rea Press, 2011), a collection of dark poetry. Her novel *Prismatic* (Lothian, 2006) won an Aurealis and her work on RPGs includes *Demon the Fallen* (White Wolf Games Studio, 2002). Short fiction, films, and plays—she's been there, as well as a whole lot of cemeteries.